ALASKA

TRAVEL GUIDE

(2023)

What You Should Know Before Your Trip, Great Places to Visit, Stunning Attractions, and Top Things to Do.

(Essential Travel Budget Tips)

Randal E. Hernandez

Copyright

TABLE OF CONTENT

WELCOME TO THE STATE OF ALASKA

Those who have a passion for the great outdoors, going on exciting excursions, and enjoying the natural beauty of the world around them will find that Alaska, the most expensive and least populated state in the United States, is an ideal area to visit. Alaska, which is located in the northwestern part of the United States, is a fascinating and captivating natural paradise that blends beautiful landscapes, abundant wildlife, and a wide variety of activities that can be enjoyed outside. This combination makes Alaska a mesmerizing natural destination. The huge topography of Alaska is home to an astonishing variety of plant and animal life, which makes it a great location for travelers wanting everything from laid-back sightseeing to adrenaline-pumping outdoor sports. During the summer months, visitors have the opportunity to indulge in a variety of activities such as hiking, camping, kayaking, fishing, and whale watching. In addition, guests have the opportunity to go to one of the nearby national parks or glaciers. During the colder months, residents and visitors to Alaska may take part in a wide variety of winter sports, including dog sledding and fishing through the ice. Besides skiing and snowboarding, other prominent winter activities include snowmobiling and snowboarding. One of the most popular tourist destinations in all of Alaska is Denali National Park, which is home to the park's namesake mountain, which also happens to be the highest point in all of North America. Denali is a destination that everybody interested in experiencing the natural magnificence of Alaska's scenery and fauna should go to at least once in their lives. The park is home to a diverse collection of animal and bird species, some of which include grizzly bears, caribou, moose, and wolves. Other inhabitants of the area include black bears. The park is home to a large number of different types of birds as well. There are a variety of outdoor activities that may be done in this location, including hiking, camping, kayaking, rafting, and just soaking in the views and sounds of the natural world. Not only is Alaska well-known for the natural beauty of its landscape, but also for the many cultural sites and attractions that can be found all around the state. Anchorage is the most populous city in the state, and as such, it offers visitors a diverse selection of activities to pick from, such as shopping, nightlife, museums, and galleries. Fairbanks is another location that sees a high number of visitors every year. This is due to the city's closeness to several hot springs as well as the wonderful views it provides of the northern lights. No matter who you are or what sort of traveler you are, Alaska has activities and sights that are enjoyable for you to experience. Because of its beautiful landscapes, many chances for outdoor activities, and rich diversity of plant and animal life, Alaska is the kind of destination that will imprint itself on your memory forever. Alaska is the place to go if you want to either have an adventure of a lifetime or get away from it all for a bit and relax. Either way, Alaska is the perfect destination for you. Come, therefore, to bask in the glory of Alaska and embark on exciting journeys through the country's last frontier.

THE VERY BEST REASONS TO GO TO ALASKA

Since there is a possibility that you will have up-close interactions with the local animals, because the landscapes are spectacular, and because there is an unlimited amount of things that may keep you occupied, Alaska has to be at the very top of your holiday wish list. The majority of people, when they think of Alaska, immediately think of snow, cold, further snow, and maybe bears. Other things that may spring to mind are bears. Alaska, on the other hand, is without a doubt one of the most breathtaking places I've ever had the opportunity to see.

You are certain to have an experience that you will never forget if you go to Alaska. You have the opportunity to immerse yourself in the historic history of the state, take in stunning vistas of the mountains, feel the grandeur of a glacier, or get up and personal with the local wildlife.

1. Views of the Region That Are Just Stunning

You are going to be astounded by the enormous range of topographic features that Alaska has to offer. Whether you travel by land, sea, or air, there is more to see than your eyes can take in; there are vast national parks, natural areas that have not been disturbed, waterfalls, majestic mountains, crystal clear lakes, glaciers, fjords, and lovely towns. There is more to see than your eyes can take in.

Even along the never-ending freeways of Alaska, there are areas to pull over and soak in the breathtaking views.

During your trip to Alaska, if you take a drive along Denali Park Road or the Seward Highway, you have a high chance of seeing wildlife such as bears, moose, whales, and eagles from the comfort of your vehicle.

2. The Wonderful Biological Diversity

There are a wide variety of animal species that call the state of Alaska their home, some of which include but are not limited to eagles, bears, caribou, moose, and otters. Denali National Park is one of the locations that provide visitors with the best possible chances of seeing them. You are allowed to drive your vehicle through the first 15 miles of the park; but, beyond that point, to continue visiting the rest of the park, you will be obliged to either walk, utilize a shuttle or bus, or ride a bike. The Denali Road Lotto, on the other hand, is held during the summer months at Denali National Park. This lottery provides visitors with the option to drive their automobiles on the roads that are located inside the park. You will have the chance to observe the "big five" creatures while you are in Denali National Park. These species are as follows: bears, Dall sheep, wolves, moose, and caribou.

3. The past and the native culture of the area

Native cultures in Alaska have had a huge effect on the way of life in the state, which can be observed in many aspects, including the architecture and art of the state's cities as well as the naming of the region's communities, mountains, and rivers. This influence can be seen everywhere. According to the most recent census conducted in the United States in 2019, Alaska has a population of little under 730,000 individuals. Of that number, 15.6% classified themselves as Native American.

4. Spectacular Glaciers

Glaciers are produced as rock debris, ice, and snow flow down from higher elevations to lower elevations and pack together to generate layers of snow. This process occurs when the rock debris, ice, and snow descend from higher elevations to lower elevations. According to estimates provided by the

Alaska Almanac, there are around 100,000 glaciers dispersed over the state of Alaska, with the Mendenhall Glacier located in Juneau being the glacier that receives the most visitors.

Several itineraries for Alaskan cruises include a stop at Glacier Bay National Park, where visitors get the chance to see glaciers breaking up into smaller pieces. The process that takes place when significant chunks of a glacier break off near the glacier's end is known as calving. You will spend the rest of your life unable to forget the incredible sight and the thunderous roar that accompanied it.

5. Unusual Experiences

But, summer is the best time to visit Alaska since the weather is more pleasant and there are more opportunities for outdoor activities. If you want to learn more about the natural world, you may participate in a wide variety of outdoor pursuits in Alaska no matter what time of year you go. You may kayak among the icebergs, explore ice caves, and cruise among the glaciers if you reserve a chartered flight and conduct some sightseeing at a higher altitude. Other activities you can participate in include exploring ice caves. Whitewater rafting, ice climbing, hiking on glaciers, and sport fishing are some of the many activities that may be enjoyed here. Why not make the most of the opportunity to mingle with natives by making the trip to one of Alaska's numerous seaside settlements and seize the chance to make new friends? You will be able to do more of the activities that are on your bucket list if you time your vacation so that it coincides with the summer months. This will allow you to take advantage of the more daylight hours. If you visit Alaska in the winter, you will increase your chances of experiencing activities like dog sledding, ice fishing, heli-skiing, and bathing in hot springs. You will also have a higher chance of witnessing the

Northern Lights. Ice fishing is another activity that may be done throughout the winter.

In addition, if you go to Alaska in the fall, you will be able to admire the vivid hues of gold, red, yellow, and purple that blanket the landscape there. This is only possible if you visit Alaska at this time. Alaska is ready to meet your need for excitement whenever you decide to visit, regardless of the time of year. All you have to do is select whatever season you want to visit during.

6. The Sun that Is Visible at Midnight

There are periods of the year in Alaska when the sun does not completely set. Beginning at the beginning of May and extending until the beginning of August, there are regions of the state where you can anticipate having sun all day or almost all day.

The latitude at which the sun will be visible above the horizon for the entire length of a 24-hour day is the Arctic Circle, which is situated 66.5 degrees north of the equator. This is the latitude at which the Arctic Circle may be found. It is feasible for towns like Fairbanks to bask in the sunlight for the whole of each waking hour since even the most southern town, Ketchikan, has 17 hours of sunshine in June. Several tour companies can take you to the Arctic Circle during the summer solstice, which is the day that is the longest of the year. In certain cities, like Fairbanks, celebrations and other late-night events are organized at various sites. A fun run, a baseball game, and Midnight Sun golf are just a few examples of these kinds of events.

7. Take some Different Paths

An Alaska road trip is one of the most entertaining ways to explore the state, and it's one of the best ways to do it. In Alaska, there are stunning vistas to be seen pretty much wherever you go and in every direction, you travel. Many people consider the roads of Alaska, such as the Denali Park Road and the Seward Highway, to be some of the most breathtaking stretches of roadway in the world. If you want to get a head start on your trip, you may start by hiring a car or an RV and traveling about. It is likely that while you are on your road trip, you will make a pit stop at the Alaska Raptor Center in Sitka to get a closer look at the bald eagles.

8. Remote Wilderness

Many people consider Alaska to be the best place in the world to go wilderness vacationing since the state is home to a multitude of protected public areas, including millions of acres, as well as three national reserves and eight national parks.

It is possible to go horseback riding in the Chugach Mountains, explore the rainforests in the Tongass National Forest, and go kayaking with the fjords and glaciers in the Kenai peninsula. Other possible activities include seeing polar bears on the tundra in the Arctic, exploring the rainforests in the Tongass

National Forest, and going horseback riding in the Arctic. If you go to Alaska, you will have the opportunity to participate in each of these activities. You have the option of going on excursions that last for a single day or many days, during which time you will stay the night in the middle of the Alaskan wilderness. There are times when getting away from the madding throng and experiencing new things is just what your spirit needs.

9. Activities that take place during the winter, such as skiing and snowboarding

Skiers and snowboarders from all over the world consider Alaska to be the skiing and snowboarding center of the world, and the state is home to a plethora of ski resorts.

CHAPTER 1

THE MOST BEAUTIFUL LOCATIONS IN ALASKA

The easiest way to identify photo-worthy landscapes in Alaska is to choose a route and begin exploring the state, but there are a few sites that truly stand out from the rest of the others. It is of the utmost importance that you remember to carry a camera with you to any one of these breathtaking areas if you plan on going there. Several instances are shown below.

1. Denali, which is located in Alaska, is a national park and preserve.

Due to the existence of valleys, glaciers, and wilderness areas totaling 6 million acres, the expansive regions around North America's tallest mountain, Denali, may be just as beautiful as the summit itself (2.4 million hectares). Along the one road that winds through the park, several amazing spots are not difficult to get to. You might, for instance, pull over at Polychrome Overlook to take in a spectacular panorama of the mountains that are all around you, or you could head to Sable Pass to keep an eye out for caribou and brown bears.

2. The Hot Springs of Chena

Even if it were situated in the middle of nothing about an hour's drive north of Fairbanks rather than in the middle of the wilderness, this resort's evergreen forest and warm thermal springs would make it one of the most beautiful places in Alaska. These features make the resort one of the most desirable places to stay in the state. But, it is also one of the best places in the world to see the Northern Lights as they dance over the night sky.

You are in the perfect spot to take in one of the most breathtaking sights in the world, as you are tucked away in the remote interior of Alaska, but you are only a short distance from the state's second-largest city. Although you are in such a remote location, you are just a short distance from Anchorage.

3. Mendenhall Glacier

Just a little distance up the road from the water is where you'll find Juneau International Airport. It is not difficult to get a car or the services of a guide who will show you around Juneau's many points of interest from the downtown region of the city. You have the option of going on Lake Mendenhall, taking a walk along the route that has been properly named the Picture Point Trail, or descending further to witness some of the most stunning landscapes in the caves that develop under the ice and which are continually changing.

4. This is the White Pass (WP)

If you find yourself in Skagway, you shouldn't forget to include some time in your itinerary to take a train ride via the White Pass and Yukon Route. This excursion is highly recommended. This railway will take you over the mountains and across the border into Whitehorse, allowing you to retrace the steps of those who participated in the Klondike Gold Rush. You will be able to take in the stunning scenery that seems to have been designed just for postcards as you go along the route.

5. Sitka

The city that was once the capital of Russian America combines the allure of the Old World with the heritage of the region's Tlingit people and the pioneering spirit of the United States. All of this is housed in a magnificent location nestled between rugged, forested islands and the mountains that are located on the Pacific coast. Climb the dormant volcano Mount Edgecumbe, discover the totem poles at Sitka National Historical Site, and keep an eye out for whales breaching in the waters around Baranof Island. At Sitka National Heritage Park, you may participate in any of these activities.

6. The Kenai Fjords National Park and Preserve is a national park in Alaska.

The Kenai Mountains are home to some of the most difficult terrain in all of Alaska, as well as some of the most stunning glaciers that can be found anywhere in the state. There is nothing quite like going on a trip to Holgate Glacier, or you could take a kayak out into Aialik Bay to get a close-up glimpse of the massive walls of ice that are there. Neither of these experiences can be compared to anything else. Be cautious around the sea lions who have made the beach their sunbathing spot. If you're up for a hike, the Harding Icefield Trail snakes its way inland, where there is a wider selection of beautiful vistas to take in along the route.

7. Hatcher Pass

This ancient mining route in the Talkeetna Mountains, which is situated to the north of Palmer, provides stunning views of the area's natural beauty and wildness. The mountain pass is marked by a variety of switchbacks, alpine lakes, and dramatic differences in height; each of these features offers the tourist a stunning new vista to take in. You may go skiing or snowmobiling and have a fantastic time in the mountains during the winter months, and during the warmer months, you can go mountain biking along the Little Susitna River. If you want to have a good time in the mountains, you should go skiing or snowmobiling.

You get the opportunity to get an up-close look at the gigantic structures that have been standing since the days of the Gold Rush by taking a tour of the Independence Mine State Historical Park. The fact that a defunct mining complex in Alaska can be one of the most beautiful sights in the surrounding area says something significant about the status of Alaska.

8. Kodiak Island

The largest island in Alaska has a lot to offer explorers, from its mountain pathways to its mountain summits, from its moss-covered woodlands to its sandy beaches. You have the option of going into the wilderness to look for brown bears among the tall Sitka spruce trees, exploring the historic buildings that are located inside the city of Kodiak, or taking in the view from Pillar Mountain. You will soon be able to participate in all of the exciting events. You have the opportunity to see whales while boating along the coast of the island or from the beaches at Miller Point, both of which are regarded as being among the most beautiful sites in all of Alaska to view whales in their natural habitat.

9. Valdez

Valdez is noted for having some of the most stunning panoramas along the Alaskan coast due to its location at the end of Prince William Sound and in a vast fjord. Valdez is also known for its historical significance. You may go kayaking among the blue icebergs in Port Valdez, or you can stroll out to one of the five adjacent glaciers. Both of these activities are available to you. You may take in the vistas of misty waterfalls flowing down cliffs by going to Shoup Bay State Marine Park, which is situated just west of the town.

10. Craig

The main city on Prince of Wales Island gives the impression of having been plopped down in the middle of a whole other world. This is because the island is home to several different biomes. The bulk of Craig's urban area is situated on a thin strip of land that is surrounded by tiny islands that are covered with flora, open water, and stunning landscape. This strip of land is located in the center of Craig. Experience the ancient woodlands of the Tongass National Forest and keep a lookout for migrating humpback whales as you travel through the region between the islands.

TOP BEACHES IN ALASKA

The state of Alaska is home to a staggering number of magnificent beaches that are excellent settings for a broad range of activities, including discovery, education, or just taking it easy and relaxing. These beaches, which may be located on either the coast of a lake or the ocean, can have a variety of different textures, ranging from gravel to sand. The beaches of Alaska are a sight to see and are often worth the trek all by themselves, regardless of whether you go to Alaska by yourself or with your family. This is true whether you travel to Alaska by yourself or with your family. Thus, you should not be hesitant! Continue reading to get information that will assist you in selecting the beach that most piques your interest, and then get ready to head off on your excursion.

1. Lowell Point in Seward, Alaska

It is possible to get to this beach by traveling to the Lowell Point Recreation site, which is a park that is 19 acres in size and is popular with those who want to kayak. It is possible to observe mountains that are covered in snow proudly projecting above Lowell Point, and below the beach, one can see a marine ecology that is prospering. After a brief excursion through the forest, one may reach the beach at their destination.

2. A visit to the beach on the Kasilof River

Beachcombing on Kasilof Beach, sightseeing, viewing wildlife, and camping are only some of the activities that are included in this package. The fee covers all of these activities. It has a commanding presence at the mouth of the Kasilof River because of its location on the Sterling River, which is about 15 miles south of Soldotna. This beach is well-known for its exceptional sport fishing opportunities for king, coho, and sockeye salmon. Anglers have the option of fishing from the shore or drift boats at this beach. The locals return here year after year to fish for salmon with dip nets, and they often set up camp to make the most of their opportunities.

3. The beach is known as Bishop's in Homer

The Island and Ocean Visitor Center is the starting point for a trip along a tiny trail that will get you to Bishop Beach, which can be found just outside of Old Town Homer on the island of Alaska. Hiking paths, a pavilion, a fire pit, a BBQ grill, picnic tables, and public art are some of the features that may be found here. In addition, the beach is just a short distance from the lodgings, restaurants, and other attractions, and can be reached in just a few minutes. Hence, even if you did not bring along sufficient provisions, all that is needed of you at this point is a brief visit to town to get some food. The breathtaking view of Lower Cook Inlet, which is further accentuated by the beach's tidal pools, is yet another one of Bishop Beach's signature characteristics. I never get sick of spending a considerable amount of time immersed in the magic of the tidal pools. An interesting experience is having the opportunity to get up close and personal with a wide variety of fish and other forms of marine life.

4. Homer Spit, Homer

Homer Spit is a narrow finger of land that juts out into Kachemak Bay and is surrounded by snow-capped mountains and glaciers. On the Homer Spit is where you'll find Homer. Visitors that come to this bustling tourist destination are guaranteed to have a good time shopping and hanging out at the beach. On the other hand, those who are interested in fishing will have the opportunity to participate in an activity that is unique here. You have the option of going on a fishing trip or giving catching salmon at The Fishin' Hole a go to see how successful you can be. After that, you will have the choice of taking the boat to Halibut Cove or spending some time exploring the many different enterprises that are situated on the spit.

5. Outside Beach, Seldovia

The boardwalk that stretches down the coast at Outside Beach is well-known, and it attracts those who take pleasure in the natural beauty that surrounds them. You may reach your destination and return via the Otterbahn Trails. Since it provides stunning vistas of both the Iliamna and the Redoubt volcanoes, this beach is an excellent option for a place to spend the night because it is close to a town. Whether you want to spend the day exploring the tidal pools, going beachcombing, or just enjoying a picnic, you are certain to have a fantastic day at this location.

6. Buskin River Beach, Kodiak Island

Kodiak City may be reached by traveling about 7.5 kilometers (4.5 miles) to Buskin River Beach. This sand and gravel beach is just a quarter of a mile long, and it may be reached by going to the Buskin River State Recreation Park. Its beaches are popular destinations for tourists who are interested in wildlife, beachcombing, and fishing. Guests have the option of spending the night at Buskin River Beach, making it a popular spot for picnics as well as overnight stays. The lush uplands of Kodiak can be seen around the coastline. For the convenience of our visitors, we have provided a Picnic Shelter that has seating for up to fifty people, is completely outfitted with amenities such as a charcoal BBQ, and even has an outhouse.

If you don't feel like roughing it for the night, you may want to consider staying at the Buskin River Inn, which is located nearby. In addition to the luxurious accommodations that they provide for guests, they also offer a dining experience that is of the highest caliber inside their institution.

7. Wasilla's Wasilla Lake Beach is located in Wasilla.

Homes in Alaska were built right on the water's edge, not too far from the Wasilla beach. Since it only goes down to a maximum depth of 14.6 meters, Wasilla Lake Beach is an excellent location for families. Because of its proximity to the highway, persons who are traveling may make use of its facilities at any time throughout their journey. The Matanuska Valley, which is situated to the east of Wasilla, is home to this beautiful lake. You will find that this location has a sandy beach that is perfect for indulging in sandcastle creation activities with your offspring. You and your children are more than welcome to make use of the picnic tables and the pavilion that is made available to you while you and your children are enjoying your time at the playground.

8. Christianson Lake in Talkeetna

The lake known as Christianson Lake is the one that is situated the farthest to the north and is the one that is considered to be the biggest of the Talkeetna Lakes. It may be found in Cook Inlet Low, which is inside the Matanuska-Susitna Borough and can be found around 1.5 miles to the east of the Talkeetna settlement. The name of the lake, which was bestowed upon it by the natives of the area, is said to have been derived from the name of a bush pilot named Haakon Christiansen who used the lake as a landing place. This lake, which covers an area of 180 acres, is perfect for swimming and wading, and it even has rainbow trout in it for the fisherman who wants to try their luck there.

9. Juneau's Eagle Beach may be found throughout the city.

The Juneau Mountains, Chilkat Mountains, and Lyn Canal can be seen from Eagle Beach, which is one of the reasons why this beach is so popular. It may be reached from Juneau by traveling north along the Glacier Highway to get there. To visit this beach, you will first need to travel to the Eagle Beach State Recreation Area, which is located nearby. It has a restroom facility in addition to a section of land that is reserved for picnics.

You will have your choice of 26 different campsites when you arrive there, three of which are walk-in sites, and five different hiking pathways. Bears have been seen on beaches, so keep a sharp watch out for them if you plan on going to one. When you have traveled to the beach, you are free to participate in any of the many activities that are common at beaches. Beachcombing and keeping an eye out for the native flora and wildlife may both now begin. Be on the lookout for a whale or some sea lions while you are on your excursion since you could find them if you keep your eyes open.

10. Petroglyph Beach in Wrangell

This rocky stretch of shore is well-known all over the world for the great historical value it has. Throughout your journey along its beaches, you will come across approximately 40 unique rock sculptures that were produced by the Tlingit people more than 8,000 years ago. Petroglyph is the word that's used to describe these carvings. In addition to this, the discovery of petroglyphs portraying salmon, whales, and maybe even human faces is a distinct possibility. In addition, Petroglyph Beach is home to a wide variety of marine life and also has a boardwalk that is perfect for walking along while taking in the sights of the surrounding area.

WILDLIFE CENTRES IN ALASKA

The majority of people who have an interest in visiting Alaska imagine the state's landscapes, including the mountains, woodlands, and animals that may be found there. There are so many fascinating animals that call Alaska home that it would be hard to list them all here. Some of these animals include moose, caribou, bears, porcupines, seals, otters, and beavers. By visiting these areas in Alaska, you will have the opportunity to witness the animals that you are interested in seeing in the most unhurried and uncomplicated way imaginable. Even Alaskans who have spent their whole lives in the state will be filled with awe and amazement when they get their first glimpse of the state's indigenous flora and fauna. You will have the highest chance of seeing wild animals if you go to one of these sites. It doesn't matter whether you've seen all there is to see or if you're excited to see your first moose; you should go to one of these areas.

1. The section of the Alaska Rainforest Sanctuary that is located in Ketchikan

This enthralling location may be hidden away in the green rainforest that surrounds Ketchikan. This rainforest is home to a wide variety of plant and animal species. This enchanting sanctuary is home to an incredible number of species, some of which include, but are not limited to, bald eagles, black bears, and banana slugs, to mention just a few examples.

2. The Musk Ox Farm may be found near Palmer, Alaska.

This property, which is situated in the Matanuska-Susitna Valley, has a surreal air. Take a visit to the gigantic musk ox, which inhabits a world of its own, and while you're there, look for scarves that are made from the very soft underfur of these animals.

3. On Admiralty Island is where you'll find the Bear's Stronghold.

If you are serious about viewing real bears from Alaska, the Fortress of the Bear is the place you should go to see them. The only thing the humans on this island can do is watch the wild animals that roam free here. Anyone can come here during the end of the summer to observe hundreds of bears gorge themselves on salmon.

4. Seward is home to the Alaska Sealife Center, which may be found throughout the city.

In the breathtaking aquarium that can be found in Seward, Alaska, you and your loved ones may enjoy a day filled with fun and excitement together. Both the decks and the tanks provide shelter for a wide variety of seabirds, and the tanks are teamed with marine life native to Alaska. During this trip, not only will everyone have a fantastic time, but they will also learn something new.

5. Wrangell's Anan Wildlife Observation Center and Visitor Center

This region is teaming with wildlife, including American bald eagles, Alaskan black bears, and brown bears, when there are significant concentrations of salmon in the river. If you want to perform some bear watching and have a chance to see these terrifying creatures of the forest, you should go to the location during the end of the summer.

6. Portage is the location of the Alaska Wildlife Conservation Center.

This remarkable conservation facility, which can be found to the south of Anchorage in the picturesque Portage Valley, allows visitors to interact with all of the animals that are indigenous to the state of Alaska. This sanctuary takes in animals who have been injured or discovered stranded and provides them with medical attention as well as a permanent home for them to live in.

7. The Alaska Zoo in Anchorage, which may be found in Anchorage

If you are unable to leave the city, you should visit the Alaska Zoo to see Alaska's native animals in an environment that is safe and safeguarded for them. Visitors get the chance to get up close and personal with animals that have been given great care at this handy location in the center of Alaska's most populated city.

CHAPTER 2

IMPORTANT FACTS YOU SHOULD KNOW

There are a lot of things you need to learn about the local flora and fauna, what you should bring with you, fascinating facts about Alaska, and other related topics before you travel to Alaska.

1. It is not feasible to see the northern lights for the whole of the year.

If seeing the Northern Lights is one of the key reasons you want to go on this trip, then you need to be aware that this phenomenon is not something that can be seen at any time of the year. Throughout the months of August through April, the northern lights may only be viewed on evenings that are very dark and with a clear sky. During the summer months, the phenomenon that is known as the midnight sun enables it to be light out for a significant portion of the night. Around the beginning of September, we were only able to get a glimpse of them, although folks had witnessed a magnificent show of the northern lights only one week before. Solar wind or solar flares must be present on the sun in addition to the aurora borealis, more widely known as the northern lights. The likelihood of seeing the northern lights may be estimated with the use of a forecast of the amount of auroral activity that will be present in the sky at any given time.

2. There are limited windows of time during which photographs of the aurora borealis are possible.

This is one of the most essential pieces of information that you need to be aware of before traveling to Alaska. It would be a bad idea to disregard this piece of advice since you may end up missing the lights as a result of doing so. The colors of the northern lights are difficult for the human eye to pick up on, but a camera can capture them beautifully. This is an advantage that photographers have. Hence, if there is a clear night, you should take images of the northern lights even if you don't think you can see them. This is because the aurora borealis is an optical illusion.

3. The entrance to Denali National Park that allows vehicles is limited to a single place in the park.

Due to the fact that it is the mountain in North America that has the greatest height, Denali is one of the most popular tourist destinations in the state of Alaska.

You probably already know this, but did you know that you can't drive on your own inside the boundaries of this national park, despite the fact that it boasts some of the most incredible mountains, trails, and views? It is common knowledge that you can pull directly into your own driveway whenever you choose. There's a good chance that this will be one of the most shocking things you find out about before traveling to Alaska. On Denali Park Road, private automobiles are only allowed to go as far as the 15-mile marker before being stopped. Once reaching that location, the bus is the sole mode of transportation available to continue your tour of the national park. The first 15 kilometers of driving through Denali National Park are well worth the time and effort because of the breathtaking landscape and the wide diversity of animals that can be seen in that area. If you want to do a tour of the park in your car, you should start there.

4. The most expensive national park in the United States is Denali National Park and Preserve, which is located in the state of Alaska. Wrangell-St. With a total land size of 13.2 million acres, Elias National Park in Alaska has the title of being the largest national park in the whole of the United States. It exceeds six times the size of Yellowstone National Park in terms of its total area. In addition to this, it is possible that all three of the national parks that are considered to be the largest in size in the United States are situated in the state of Alaska. The Wrangell-St. Elias National Park and Preserve is home to a number of glaciers, an abundance of various animal species, and one of the highest peaks in the United States. The National Park of Elias.

5. The rain falls and stops in unpredictable succession.

Since it is famously impossible to foresee the weather in Alaska, you should always come prepared for everything that may occur. Maintain a state of readiness at all times for the prospect of precipitation, but try not to place too much weight on the weather forecast since it may change at the drop of a hat. The quantity of precipitation that falls on the state of Alaska varies substantially depending on the location as well as the time of year due to the fact that Alaska is the largest state in the United States. May is normally the month in the state that receives the least amount of rainfall, while September is often the month that receives the most. However, if you are going to go on a vacation, it is highly recommended that you bring rain gear with you, regardless of the time of year.

6. It is advisable to dress in layers since there is a chance that the weather may be unpredictable.

As was said before, it is notoriously difficult to accurately anticipate the weather in Alaska. It's possible that the day may start off warm and sunny, but then turn cold and cloudy later on. When the weather report calls for a range of possible circumstances, the most prudent course of action is to dress in layers. If you find that you are becoming too hot, you may quickly take off your jacket. If, on the other hand, you allow yourself to grow chilly, you won't be able to conjure anything up out of thin air. Wool socks are another piece of gear that you really need to bring with you if you are going to be hiking in rainy weather or if you are going to be traveling during a more chilly time of year. Cotton takes longer to dry than other fabrics, and once it gets wet, the problems it causes are compounded by the fact that it can absorb and retain water in its structure.

7. You really must always have rain gear on hand, both for yourself and for your camera.

Rain is rather typical in Alaska, and as a consequence, I cannot stress enough the need of bringing appropriate rain gear to ensure not only your comfort but also your safety. Being wet is never a pleasant experience; however, staying wet while it is cold outdoors is a far more terrible experience than getting wet in the first place.

8. Around eight o'clock in the evening, the bulk of the restaurants are no longer open for business.

Take into consideration that many of the restaurants in Alaska close as early as 8:00 p.m. when you are in the process of organizing your next holiday. If you want to eat later for dinner but still go out to eat in Alaska, you will need to do some research to make sure that restaurants are still open at the time you want to eat at them.

9. There is a possibility that the prices of meals at Alaskan restaurants may become too expensive.

If you are traveling on a limited budget, it is imperative that you familiarize yourself with the following information before going to Alaska. Since Alaska is located in such a distant part of the United States, importing food into the state may be a challenging task at times. As a consequence of this, the cost of food at restaurants, particularly the cost of quick service restaurants, may be much more than it would be in the contiguous United States. You shouldn't let this discourage you from trying some of the incredible cuisines that Alaska has to offer because, of course, you should. But, you should make the necessary preparations, and you should also be prepared to spend a little bit more than you had anticipated.

10. There are some stunning perspectives to be had along the roads thanks to the landscape.

It's probable that the fact that driving is a popular activity among Alaskans may come as somewhat of a shock to you when you find out about it. Since the panoramas are so stunning, you don't even have to get out of your car to take in some of the most spectacular scenery in the world. You can do it all from the comfort of your own vehicle. Whether you are beginning your adventure in Anchorage, which is a wonderful place to do so, selecting the Glenn Highway, the Parks Highway, or the Seward Highway for your scenic drive is a decision you just cannot go wrong with. Don't forget to carry your camera with you everywhere you go.

11. While traveling over a long distance by automobile, portable battery packs are an absolute need.

The last thing you want to be worrying about while you are out on the open road soaking in the views is whether or not your phone will maintain its charge. You should make it a habit to have a mobile phone charger with you wherever you go behind the wheel of a vehicle. This will allow you to avoid any problems that may arise as a direct consequence of being without a phone. While paper maps of the area are a helpful tool to have, you should instead have a vehicle charger with you.

12. It is possible to travel a considerable distance before reaching the next gas station.

While planning a road trip throughout Alaska, it is crucial to ensure that there will be enough access to a sufficient number of gas stations along the route. This is especially important for longer stretches of the journey. Even though there are a few of them, you won't find too many gas stations in many parts of Alaska, notably in the area that extends between

Valdez and Fairbanks, but there are several. When traveling to Alaska, it is very important to be aware of the fact that cell phone service is not always consistent across the state. This is one of the most important pieces of information you will need. And if you are thinking about driving on the Dalton Highway, which is frequently considered to be Alaska's most desolate roadway, you should be aware that there is a 240-mile stretch of the road that does not have any gas stations along it. If you are planning on driving on the Dalton Highway, you should be aware of this fact.

13. Highways and other important roadways almost always have some kind of work going on beside them.

In the mountainous parts of Alaska, it is not uncommon for there to be a need for road repair. This is due to the fact that the state's highways are constantly getting battered up by the elements, notably precipitation, and wind. While road construction is being done, which takes place the majority of the time in the summer, one-lane routes might have occasional traffic jams as a consequence of the work. Hence, if you are driving in Alaska, you shouldn't be surprised if you run into any kind of traffic at any point. It won't be difficult at all to discover things to do in order to pass the time while you wait when you take into consideration how breathtaking the scenery is.

14. The term "contiguous United States" is used in Alaska to refer to the 48 states that are located south of the state of Alaska.

It is likely that the first time you hear someone refer to the contiguous United States as the Lower 48 you will be perplexed by the statement; nonetheless, this is a term that is often used by people who are originally from Alaska. If you want to give the impression to the locals that you have a solid grasp of Alaskan jargon, this is a term that you should definitely be acquainted with.

15. Bears of both the brown and black varieties are known to inhabit Alaska in significant numbers.

Bears of both black and brown kids are numerous in Alaska, giving the state a total bear population that is substantially more robust than that of the majority of the other states in the United States. In spite of their conventional moniker, black bears may really have fur that ranges in hue from a light golden brown to a bluish-gray. When compared to black bears, brown bears are often much bigger, have a more pronounced hump on their backs, and have claws that are much longer. These are the most notable distinctions that can be noticed between their physical appearances. It is more probable to come across a brown bear along the water's edge, while a black bear will be discovered in the forest.

Although it is very unlikely that a bear would attack a human, you should still keep your distance if you come across one when you're outside.

16. Grizzly bears are members of the family of bears known as brown bears.

There is a possibility of seeing brown bears and black bears in their native environment in the state of Alaska. You should know that grizzly bears are a subspecies of brown bears if you're wondering about the role that grizzly bears play in the overall scheme of things. The fact that grizzly bears are more common in mountainous locations than brown bears is the most significant difference between the two species. Brown bears are more likely to be found in coastal areas. In addition to this, brown bears are much larger than grizzly bears. Regardless of whether or not this information is common knowledge in the United States, having it on hand is quite helpful when making plans for a trip to Alaska because of the many opportunities it presents.

17. When it comes to watching black bears, the best time of year is from June through September.

In Alaska, the months of June and September provide the best opportunities to see bears. This is mostly due to the fact that this is the time of year when the salmon runs are at their strongest. From the end of May through the month of July, bears are in the thick of the mating season, which also happens to coincide with the season for salmon. So, throughout this time period, there will be a greatly enhanced possibility of coming across at least one or two bears. If you want to enhance your chances of viewing bears in a setting that is both safe and fantastic, it is definitely worth it to pay the about $15 to $18 entry price to visit the Alaska Wildlife

Conservation Center. The center is located in Anchorage, Alaska.

TRANSPORTATION OPTIONS TO GET TO ALASKA

How do I get to Alaska?

It is possible to go to Alaska through a variety of various means of transport, such as flying, traveling by boat, or traveling by car. By a wide margin, the most time-efficient method is to fly into Anchorage; hence, this is also the most popular one.

Flying to Alaska is a viable option for vacationers.

Anchorage is the most important transportation hub in the state of Alaska, and as the state's largest city, it is serviced by flights from a number of the world's most well-known airlines, including United, American, Delta, and Alaska Airlines. Several cities, such as Chicago, Minneapolis, Denver, Los Angeles, and Seattle, provide direct travel options to this destination. Moreover, it is possible to fly into Fairbanks or Juneau; however, these airports are much smaller and have fewer daily flights than Anchorage International Airport. For more information, kindly visit the section of our site that is devoted to flights to Alaska.

To go to Alaska, you will need to use a boat service.

A broad range of outlying communities in Southeast Alaska is only connected to one another via the efforts of the Alaska State Ferry, which plays an important role in this process. In addition, the ferry operates a route that begins in Bellingham, Washington, and serves as a link between Alaska and the lower 48 states. This route travels northward. It takes more than 36 hours to get to Alaska, but it's a beautiful journey, and since the ferry can accept automobiles, it's a unique option for a holiday in which you drive yourself throughout Alaska. Since the ferry can accept automobiles, it's a beautiful option for a holiday in which you drive yourself throughout Alaska. Please go to the page on our website that is dedicated to the Alaska State Ferry for more information.

Although passengers on one-way glacier route cruises that depart from Vancouver are able to achieve this goal, the great majority of passengers do not first consider boarding a cruise as a means to go to Alaska. Your cruise will most likely conclude in Seward or Whittier, both of which are wonderful places from which to undertake a post-cruise land tour of Alaska. If you are traveling in a northerly direction, your cruise will most likely end in Seward.

Instructions for Those Who Want to Drive to Alaska

Automobile travel is an option for getting to Alaska from the lower 48 states. The majority of passengers enter Canada from the north in order to connect with the Alaska Highway, sometimes referred to as the "Alcan." This route spans the whole of the nation, beginning in Dawson Creek in British Columbia and ending in Delta Junction in Alaska. There is no bus or motorcoach service that connects Alaska to the states that make up the rest of the United States that are considered to be the continental United States.

You can go to Alaska by rail if you really want to. We are asked very often, "Is there a train to Alaska?" which is an interesting issue to ponder. There is a reputable rail service inside the state of Alaska; however, there is no train service that operates from the United States mainland into

Alaska. You are necessary to have a current passport in order to go to Alaska since your route there will take you through Canada. This is true regardless of whether you get there by flying, going on a cruise, or driving.

MONTH BY MONTH IN ALASKA

JANUARY

Spend days leading up to the New Year in Alaska, where you can view the northern lights, go skiing or ice skating, and maybe even go dog sledding. The city of Anchorage is home to a strong arts scene and a number of cultural organizations. The well-known Anchorage Folk Festival keeps the city active, while Alaska Beer Week stirs up excitement over the region's most cherished specialty brews. Both of these events take place in Anchorage. Anchorage is the location of each of these events. Take a ride on the Alaska Railroad to Hurricane Turn for stunning views of snow-capped Denali, or hop on a helicopter to get a bird's-eye view of Chugach State Park and its beautiful glaciers. Both of these experiences are really once-in-a-lifetime opportunities.

Temperatures tend to hover in the low 20s throughout the month of January, and there are less than six hours of daylight on average each day. Because of this, the nights are crisp and last for a long time, making them a great time to enjoy the beautiful views of the aurora that the city has to offer.

FEBRUARY

When miners and fur trappers from Alaska would come up to the city after a long winter's work to celebrate the end of the season, Fur Rondy became a custom in Anchorage. This tradition goes back to the early days of the municipality of Anchorage when it was first established. The annual Fur Rondy competition takes place throughout the month of February. These days, the celebration lasts for two weeks and includes a parade, a fireworks display, a carnival, and a variety of other activities that are unique to Alaska, such as the World Championship Sled Dog Races and the world-famous Running of the Reindeer. In addition, the celebration also includes a variety of other activities that can only be found in Alaska. The rest of this month will be spent participating in some of Alaska's most popular outdoor pursuits, such as snowshoeing, dog sledding, skiing, and searching for the northern lights.

MARCH

The end of Fur Rondy and the beginning of the Iditarod take place at the same time, making the month of March the ideal time to cheer on some of the most talented canine athletes in the world as they make their way to Nome in Alaska. Before the beginning of The Last Great Race, a ceremony will take place on Fourth Avenue in the middle of downtown Anchorage. The whole city will be filled with merriment and enthusiasm for the upcoming event. When the teams have left, visitors to Anchorage in March may be able to enjoy activities such as skiing in the spring, visiting arts and cultural destinations, and seeing the return of gray whales migrating north from Baja. These are just some of the options available to them (make sure to book a day trip cruise through Resurrection Bay).

APRIL

The annual Slush Cup held at Alyeska Resort makes the most of the snow that is still on the slopes by having skiers compete to see who can jump the farthest over a pond that has been frozen solid, much to the pleasure of the spectators. The month of April in Anchorage represents the beginning of spring, and this event makes the most of the snow that is still on the mountains at that point in time. Around this time, the Alaska Wildlife Conservation Center and other locations around town are seeing a growing number of newborn animals for the first time. The NYO Games is a celebration of traditional Alaska Native sports and activities that are full of a lot of fun. Towards the end of this month, some of the top athletes in the state will gather in Anchorage to participate in the NYO Games.

MAY

May is a wonderful month to visit Anchorage because it is when the city's well-known red Anchorage Trolley Tours and other sightseeing excursions begin departing daily from downtown when glacier cruises begin sailing Portage Lake and Prince William Sound, and when king salmon begin running in Ship Creek. All of these activities contribute to May being one of the most beautiful months in Anchorage.

JUNE

The flowers in Town Square Park are starting to blossom, fishermen are gathering at Ship Creek for the annual Slam'n Salmon Festival, and Alaskans are getting ready to celebrate the Summer Solstice with activities like baseball, a carnival, live music, picnics, and other enjoyable events. At Chugach State Park, the towering peaks and rolling valleys are a favorite destination for hikers, while in Anchorage, the municipal lakes are popular locations for paddlers to enjoy the outdoors (try a kayak, stand-up paddleboard, or canoe).

JULY

The month of July in Alaska is traditionally known for hosting many of the state's most well-liked summer festivals, and it is also a month that is filled with opportunities for the whole family to have a good time. After attending a jam-packed day of activities such as the Fourth of July celebration in Anchorage, the annual Bear Paw Festival, and the Girdwood Forest Fair, take some time to unwind by going on a hike, riding a bike, fishing, or going flightseeing. July is the best month for doing everything you want to do.

AUGUST

The month of August marks the beginning of the berry season in Anchorage, and around this time of year, the blueberry patches that run along the Chugach State Park mountain sides grow very thick and lush. The city's hiking pathways and urban greenspaces are full of berry pickers dragging buckets and baskets during this time of year because of the annual Blueberry Festival that is hosted in Alyeska Resort. This event is a fun-filled opportunity to appreciate the delicious harvest. The celebration takes place once a year in July.

SEPTEMBER

During the month of September, when the fall colors first start to show over the landscape, the Anchorage Bowl transitions from being green to having hues of gold, crimson, and bronze. This happens when the ground is covered in snow. The enormous moose population in the area has started to rut now that the mating season has begun, and the animals have started to congregate in the city in order to get ready for the next winter. This creates ideal conditions for anyone interested in wildlife photography and observation (just be sure to keep a safe distance). Meanwhile, municipal hiking and biking trails continue to be popular destinations for those who wish to take advantage of the fact that the ground is not yet covered with snow while appreciating the fall foliage.

OCTOBER

When October's skies are clear, photographers and viewers flock to the city of Anchorage and the surrounding area in hopes of catching sight of the Northern Lights. There are a number of scenic places in and around the city. There are a lot of different ways to fish for rainbow trout, as well as other colorful activities, including Oktoberfest, fall sightseeing and animal watching, and other seasonal activities. Visitors to Alaska have the opportunity to participate in activities that are unique to the state at any hour of the day or night.

NOVEMBER

The first snowfall in the city often occurs around the month of November. This marks the beginning of the winter season in Alaska, which is prime time for various winter activities, including skiing, snowmobiling, snowshoeing, dog sledding, and many more. Keep warm by eating locally produced delicacies and drinking craft beverages at some of Anchorage's top restaurants and breweries. Enjoy the world-class cross-country trails of Anchorage. Drive to Alyeska Resort or Arctic Valley to hit the downhill ski slopes with breathtaking vistas of Chugach State Park.

DECEMBER

The days leading up to Christmas in Anchorage are jam-packed with a wide range of thrilling events, such as dazzling city nights, illuminating northern lights, adrenaline-pumping winter sports, and cozy community get-togethers. You may rent ice skates and glide over the hot-mopped surface of Westchester Lagoon, see the famous tree-lighting ritual in Town Square Park, sing carols with the audience at Anchorage's annual Tuba Christmas performance, or stare up at the New Year's Eve fireworks that are shown above Ship Creek.

Anchorage is home to each and every one of these pursuits and pastimes.

CHAPTER 3

GETTING AROUND ALASKA

Travel Options Available in Alaska

It turns out that Alaska provides a wide range of possibilities for vacations—possibly even more than you could have hoped for or imagined. Several variables contribute to this, including Alaska's enormous size and the creative strategies that are used to transport people and goods around the state. There are also several good modes of public transportation accessible to visitors, however, these options are not always available in every place.

Getting Around the State of Alaska By Automobile

Like with the vast majority of other places in the United States, driving is the best way to get about in Alaska. But, there are more opportunities, which I will elaborate on in the following paragraphs.

A hired automobile

In Alaska, renting a car is the most time- and cost-efficient mode of transportation. My opinion is that it is the least difficult since it provides you with the most liberty and adaptability, which is the primary reason why so many people go to Alaska in the first place. If your idea of a wonderful vacation includes a lot of traveling (Alaska is a large state; plan on at least an hour of driving to get from one place to another!) You might want to consider renting a vehicle for most or all of your journey in Alaska if you want to be able to stop whenever you want to appreciate the wildlife and take in the scenery.

In Alaska, you may rent a car from any of the major firms, however, the prices may vary somewhat depending on where in the state you go to make your reservation. You may also try your luck with local car rental companies or with the online marketplace Turo if you're having problems obtaining a vehicle.

RV/Motorhome

Traveling around Alaska in a recreational vehicle (RV) is yet another popular option. There is no need to make hotel bookings, which is a terrific advantage if you want the flexibility to not even know where you'll stay each night if you hire an RV. Nevertheless, renting an RV is more expensive than renting a car. It is permissible to camp, commonly known as boondocking, in Alaska; but, if you want to spend the night in or near a particular municipality, you should learn the rules governing overnight stays there beforehand. In addition, there are several Alaska State Parks that provide connections for RVs and facilities for pumping out waste.

Driving a recreational vehicle (RV) in Alaska is typically not too difficult, especially one of the smaller 25-foot RVs that are often offered as rental vehicles in the state. There is a possibility that you may have problems finding parking places; thus, it is imperative that you research the activities that you want to participate in, especially those that take place in towns, and establish direct contact with them if required to confirm that they provide RV parking.

Private Automobile

While traveling to Alaska, you have the option of either driving your vehicle or making use of the Alaska Marine Highway System. (I get into the topic of the ferry in further detail below.)

There is just one road that can take you to Alaska, and that road is the Alaska-Canadian Highway (commonly known as the ALCAN). It starts in Dawson Creek, British Columbia, and ends in Delta Junction, Alaska. Nevertheless, it takes a much longer trip to get to Dawson Creek from the Lower 48, and it takes much longer to get from Delta Junction to Fairbanks or Anchorage. The road was initially established in 1942 and has a total distance of 1,387 miles. Be prepared for long days on the road; the average time it takes people to drive the trip is between five and seven days, although that varies depending on how much they stop and see along the way.

Transportation around Alaska is Provided by Bus

You can get throughout Alaska by taking a bus if you don't want to drive yourself, don't want to go by another route, or if your trip budget won't allow you to do so.

The Connection to Central Park

We are very fortunate that there is now a bus route linking the major cities in Alaska. This makes it possible for those who are unable to drive, use trains, or fly to still have the opportunity to see the state. Seward, which is located inside Kenai Fjords National Park, Anchorage, and Denali are all served by the Park Link bus service, which makes many stops along the way (in the Denali National Park). Every day, the bulk of buses go between Anchorage, Denali, and Seward, and the timetables are designed to make it easy to transfer between the different routes. The cost of a one-way ticket for an adult ranges from $70 to $140.

Tour groups

Some people choose to go to Alaska by participating in a tour with other people, which often includes taking the bus at some point during the journey. Bus and motorcoach excursions are a typical way to tour the state without having to drive or worry about the practicalities of the trip. The majority of the large cruise lines provide these excursions as add-on options for passengers.

Buses from Denali Park

It would be irresponsible of me to include the Denali park buses from our discussion since they are the most well-known buses in Alaska. These are the only two methods that visitors may get into Denali National Park since the park does not allow private automobiles.

Although the majority of pick-up and drop-off places may be found in and around Nenana Canyon, these spots often do not connect you from one place to another. Despite this, many provide transportation to and from Kantishna for those who are staying in the area for a long period.

Taking the Train in the Great Land of Alaska

While you make preparations for your trip on the Alaska Railroad, you may notice the distinctive blue and gold rail carriages that make up the railroad. I often recommend it to people who are coming to Alaska for the first time since it is a once-in-a-lifetime opportunity and the only commercial train line in the state. Since it takes a route that is distinct from that of the highway system, the experience that you have will be distinct from that which you have when driving.

Getting Around Alaska by Using an Airplane

If you need to go from one region to another, there are two options available to you: commercial airplanes, which are often offered by Alaska Airlines, or bush planes. Unless you're going to one of Alaska's most remote national parks, southwest Alaska, or the Arctic, you won't typically need a bush plane for your trip across the Last Frontier state of the United States of America.

Anchorage, Fairbanks, Juneau, Sitka, and Ketchikan are among the main cities and medium-sized villages in Alaska that provide a variety of commercial services. In addition, there are flights to numerous other smaller settlements, including Cordova, Yakutat, Petersburg, Wrangell, Kodiak, King Salmon, Nome, Kotzebue, and Prudhoe Bay. Utqiagvik is also serviced by these airlines (Barrow). There is no need to be concerned if the second set of destinations does not seem to be recognizable to you since first-time visitors seldom travel there.

A flightseeing aircraft is another alternative for traveling around Alaska by air. Nevertheless, as these aircraft often pick passengers up and drop them off at the same location, a flightseeing tour does not just consist of moving from one location to another. The Glacier Landing in Denali National Park (departing from Healy) with Fly Denali and the Katmai National Park Bear Watching with Rust's Flight Service are two of the most popular flightseeing excursions that I recommend to my clients. Both of these tours are offered by Rust's Flight Service (from Anchorage).

Exploring Alaska by Boat

According to a widely circulated statistic, the state of Alaska has more miles of coastline than the whole of the United States put together. This indicates that people who live in Alaska as well as visitors often make use of boats and other types of marine transportation to move about the state. These are the options available to you.

Ships That Provide Daylong Cruises

A cruise is an excellent method to get to know Southeast Alaska since the region is only accessible by air and not by vehicle. Boating is the greatest way to take in the scenery and explore some of the settlements in this region, which is often referred to as the Inner Passage due to the huge network of canals and a large number of islands in the area.

The three basic categories of cruise ships are mega-ships (carrying 2,500 passengers or more), mid-sized ships (carrying between 500 and 1,500 people), and small ships (carrying less than 150 people). The majority of big and medium-sized ships in the fleet operate one-way voyages between southern ports like Vancouver and Seattle and northern terminals like Seward and Whittier. These cruises typically depart from the southern port. You have the option of sailing either north or south, but I would recommend that you go in the other direction and add at least five more days to your trip so that you may see the rest of Alaska on land.

The Alaska Marine Highway and Transportation System

If you like the idea of seeing Alaska by water but aren't interested in taking a cruise ship, the Alaska Marine Highway System, also known as the Alaska State Ferry, is a much less formal alternative that you may take if you want to see the state. The ferry is an essential element of the transportation system in Alaska, especially for the small communities in Southeast and Southwest Alaska that are cut off from the mainland by a lack of roads. The majority of the large seashore communities in these regions are linked by ferries, including Juneau, Sitka, Ketchikan, Whittier, and Kodiak, amongst others. It is a mode of travel throughout the state that does not include any frills and is only marginally more cost-effective than taking a trip on a ship with many more bells and whistles.

Tours of Boat Major Maritime Areas

If you genuinely appreciate being on the water, there are alternative ways to get about Alaska that include boats. These cruises, much like flightseeing, don't allow you to travel between destinations, but they do provide you access to parts of Alaska that would otherwise be unavailable to you. If you wanted to hire a boat to check anything off your Alaska bucket list, you could also lease one for the day (such as a fishing charter) or use it as transportation.

Options Available for Alaska's Public Transportation

While there aren't many options for public transportation in Alaska, I thought I'd share some information with you nevertheless just in case you were curious. If you just plan to visit the state's main cities, you may easily go across the state without renting a car by using public transportation like the Park Link bus, the Alaska Railroad train system, or even flying between cities.

In a nutshell, public transportation is restricted to the city centers of the world. For instance, you can use the bus to go about inside Anchorage and even Fairbanks. Also, there is a bus line that connects Anchorage to Eagle River and the Mat-Su Valley, both of which are places where I spent my childhood (Palmer and Wasilla). Nevertheless, as you will see, traveling by car is not required to see any of the top five tourist destinations in Alaska.

Anchorage Public Transit for Those Without a Car

The Anchorage People Mover bus system is very dependable, even though the vast majority of residents in the city do not make use of public transit. The schedules worked out well for me, and I had no issue getting the bus from downtown Anchorage to South Anchorage to check out the new location of the Anchorage Market. The bus is the most economical option given that a ride just costs $2. Taxis and ride-sharing services such as Uber and Lyft are also available in Anchorage, even though their rates are much higher. On the other hand, the cost of the same journey by Uber to the Anchorage Market was estimated to be $38.

Transportation in Fairbanks for Those Who Don't Have a Car

Since it is so comparable to Anchorage in this sense, it is possible to navigate about Fairbanks without the need for a car. Using any one of the eight different bus lines, you may go to the North Pole, the Museum of the North (which is located on the campus of the University of Alaska Fairbanks), and the airport (denoted by their color).

Even though Fairbanks is just around one-tenth the size of Anchorage, the number of taxis and car-sharing services available there is far lower. You shouldn't count on this as a mode of transportation unless it's an absolute last resort.

Denali's Method of Transportation That Doesn't Include a Car

A significant number of travelers are afraid that they won't be able to go around Denali without a car if they use the Alaska Railroad to get there. You shouldn't be concerned for the following two reasons:

First things first: there are shuttles available for everything. You name it, we provide shuttle service for hotels and amusement parks. If you indicate that you will be using the train to go to Denali, the hotel will provide a shuttle service and inquire about your interest in utilizing it when you make your reservation.

Second, the business center of Denali, which consists of hotels and dining establishments, is not very large. It is not difficult to walk from one end of the Nenana Canyon/Glitter Gulch area to the other.

How to Travel About Seward If You Don't Have a Vehicle

In the same way that this is the situation with Denali, some people go to Seward in Anchorage by train and worry that they won't be able to get about the town without a car. While Seward is not as small as Denali, it is still possible to view practically everything in Seward within a walking distance of the railway terminal and port, which is the central location of the town.

What to Do If You Don't Have a Car: Suggestions for Getting About Seward

Others take the train from Anchorage to Seward in the same way that they go to Denali, and they worry that they won't be able to get about the town without using a car. Although Seward is not as tiny as Denali, it is still possible to view practically everything in Seward within walking distance of the railway terminal and port. Denali is the more compact of the two towns. Denali is the smaller of the two towns, making it the more convenient option.

What to Do If You Don't Have a Car in Juneau and Want to Go About the City

Since it is more similar to Seward than it is to Fairbanks in terms of its geography, Juneau is another city that could make you feel anxious if you attempt to move about without using a car. Although larger, Juneau is a more compact city than Fairbanks. Although the Juneau airport is situated a fair distance from the heart of the city, several hotels in the vicinity provide shuttle service. In addition, there are other fallback options available in the form of car-sharing programs, taxi services, and the Capital Transit bus system. Because the majority of Juneau's tourist attractions and activities are located within easy walking distance of the city center, it is possible to take advantage of virtually all of the city's offerings without having to rent or operate a vehicle. This is because the majority of Juneau's attractions and activities for visitors are located within easy walking distance of the city center.

The Easiest and Most Time-Effective Way to Travel Across Alaska

The issue that has to be answered is, what is the best time- and cost-effective way to travel around Alaska? In my opinion, the most interesting and fun way to see Alaska is to travel across the state using a mix of the many forms of transportation available. A terrific trip to Alaska will include sightseeing from the air, some time spent driving (or riding) in a bus or train, and at least one day spent on a cruise. In any event, if you want to see most of Alaska on your trip, the route that I suggest choosing is the one that has the highest foot traffic.

Beyond that, the ideal method to move about Alaska is the one that fits with your schedule, compliments the way you want to travel, and is reasonable within the travel budget you have set up for your trip. As I indicated at the beginning of this paragraph, the choice of whatever method(s) of transportation you would want to utilize while you are in Alaska is totally up to you. You may fly, drive, take the train, or take the ferry. My posts on itineraries will often contain my advice and recommendations, but in the end, the choice is entirely up to you.

CHAPTER 4

SUMMERTIME IN ALASKA

When it comes to places to visit during the summer, Alaska is home to a number of alternatives that are among the very best. In Alaska, the potential for you to have a good time and get a genuine adrenaline rush is, quite literally, without bounds. The following is a list of things that may be done in Alaska during the summertime that is fun for the whole family.

1. You will arrive in Whittier after driving through a memorial tunnel that honors Anton Anderson.

This highway tunnel is the only one ever built anywhere in the world to be able to withstand temperatures as low as -40 degrees Fahrenheit and speeds as high as 150 miles per hour. With a length of 2.5 miles, it is the longest highway tunnel in all of North America.

2. Attend the Mountain Marathon Run in Seward on the Fourth of July to get in the holiday spirit.

Mt. Marathon organizes a footrace that takes place every year on the fourth of July, and the charming town of Seward serves as the venue for the event.

This footrace has a distance of three miles round-trip and an ascent of a mountain that is 3022 feet above sea level. There are around 700 runners who take part in the competition. The ascent comes to an end after a distance of a little less than one mile. During the Olympic Games, millions of people from all over the world travel to the host city to take part in the festivities, watch the competitions, and cheer on their favorite athletes. You can be certain that taking part in this activity will be one of the highlights of your time spent in Alaska during the summer.

3. You may try out ziplining at Icy Strait Point, which is located near Hoonah.

We would like to use this opportunity to welcome you to the longest zip line journey in the world! This ride on the zipline at Icy Strait Point is unlike anything else you have ever experienced, and it is without a doubt a once-in-a-lifetime chance that will have you yelling with excitement. You won't have the chance to see something like this anywhere else other than in Alaska.

4. Take part in a Hiking Trip with a Guide That Will Take You Around the Glaciers

Across the whole of the last frontier, you have a vast range of options from which to choose one at your discretion. Get the services of a reliable local guide in the region that you are currently in and get up close and personal with these breathtaking land masses. The chance to go on an adventure in the great outdoors in Alaska is really remarkable.

5. Experience the thrill of flying above Mount McKinley, the highest peak on the continent of North America.

Go to the skies with a reputable flight-seeing company that will take you on excursions that take you all around Denali, the mountain peak that is the highest point in all of North America.

6. In the region of Halibut Cove, guests have the opportunity to experience a live floating amphitheater, live music ranging from blues to bluegrass, excellent food, plentiful wine, and the warm friendliness that is characteristic of Alaska. This event's whole revenues will be donated to the Homer Foundation in the amount of one hundred percent. Every feeling imaginable! A wonderful experience during a magnificent Alaskan summer.

7. . Explore the El Capitan Cave by going to Prince of Wales Island and doing so.

El Capitan Cave, which can be located in the Tongass National Forest, holds the record for being the longest cave in Alaska that has been explored and mapped. Individuals who go on an in-depth investigation of this matter may have to travel more than two miles. This amazing cavern may be explored, but only when the weather is warmer. You will have to plan your trip accordingly. The U.S. Forest Service offers free of charge narrated hikes all around the forest. It is without a doubt one of the most delightful summer activities that can be participated in across the state of Alaska.

8. Make it a point to check out The Salty Dawg.

The walls and ceiling of this historic bar in Homer are covered with dollar bills that have been left behind by previous patrons. If you've made it to the Salty Dawg, you may as well spend the night on the Homer Spit and take a stroll down the boardwalk to see the many works of art, shops, restaurants, and other businesses that cater to tourists.

9. Attend the Alaska Day festivities in Sitka this year.

Sitka served as the location for the Purchase Transfer of the Russian claim to Alaska to the United States of America on October 18, 1867. In commemoration of this momentous occasion, the Alaska Day Celebration is conducted annually in Sitka. This festival pays homage to the many historical perspectives and cultural customs that have been practiced in Alaska for generations.

10. See the Grizzly Bear Stronghold while you're in town.

If you happen to be in Sitka already, you may as well take the short drive down the road and have a look at this breathtaking area while you're there. The Fortress of the Bear is an animal refuge that provides rescued animals with safety and care, in addition to providing them with an environment that is engaging and educational for the animals. They have made it their mission to seek out and rescue cubs that have been harmed, nurse them back to health, and watch after their well-being to ensure that they have long and productive lives.

11. Relax and rejuvenate in the spa and natural hot springs at the Chena Resort.

In the middle of the scorching summer, thermal springs? Exactly, and I don't see why not. Due to the fact that we are in Alaska, the manner in which things are carried out here is a little bit different. In addition to a heated indoor pool, hot tubs, an ice museum, and a massage center, the list of available facilities also includes hot springs that may be found on the property itself. If you are searching for activities to do in Alaska during the summer, you should put this site at the top of your list since it is so stunning.

12. Prepare Your Tent for the Night in the Woods

It makes little difference precisely where you are inside Alaska's vast territory, which spans a total of 663,300 kilometers. Just getting away from the chaos of the city and taking in the sights and smells of nature may do wonders for your mental and physical well-being. There are 6,640 miles of coastline in Alaska, so we are certain that you will be able to find a spot that is appropriate for camping anywhere in the state.

13. Visit An Ice Cave

There are a handful of these hidden diamonds stashed away throughout Alaska, and you can find them everywhere from Juneau to the MatSu Valley to the Kenai Peninsula. These jewels may be discovered in a variety of settings. These are the kinds of sites that locals and visitors alike could enjoy. Remember to use the utmost caution at all times, even if it might be an exhilarating experience since these areas have the potential to become highly dangerous.

14. Travel Throughout the State of Alaska aboard the Alaska Railroad.

Taking the historic Alaska Railroad from Seward to Whittier and further north via Denali National Park and into Fairbanks is a fantastic way to see Alaska with zero interruptions other than observing animals and the gleaming mountains. This route can be taken from Seward to Whittier and further north via

Denali National Park and into Fairbanks. You may get further information on the many itineraries, schedules, and costs that the Alaska Railroad offers by going to their website.

15. Enjoy the crisp air and the sun that doesn't set until after midnight by going on a trek.

Because there is nothing that says "I'm in Alaska" quite like going on a trek in the middle of the night when there are no stars visible in the sky above you. This is because it is one of the most iconic things that visitors do when they come to Alaska. Hiking in Alaska is without a doubt one of the most pleasurable methods to get familiar with the state of Alaska.

WINTERTIME IN ALASKA

Despite this, a vacation to Alaska during the winter might end up being one of the most memorable and enriching experiences of your whole life. Taking a trip to Alaska in the winter is a fantastic way to travel in an environmentally responsible manner while simultaneously making a positive contribution to the development of the regional economy. And now, for your perusal, here is a list of what we believe to be some of the most enjoyable things to do in Alaska during the winter season.

1. Experience the breathtaking phenomenon of the Northern Lights.

The month of March in Alaska, which begins in the middle of September and lasts until the end of April, is when you will have the highest chance of seeing the Northern Lights. The region of Alaska that is between 65 and 70 degrees North Latitude will provide the greatest opportunity for you to see one of these animals.

2. Dog Mushing

Dog sledding with huskies is a popular activity in Alaska during the winter months.

The state of Alaska has a long tradition of dog sledding, and the state is also the location of the Iditarod Sled Dog Race, which is known all over the world. Since there are so many different outfitters in the area, you will be able to go dog sledding as long as there is snow as long as you book your excursion in advance. You should generally be able to plan a vacation from the middle of October to somewhere around the middle of April, however, this will depend on the part of the state you are going to. By taking a trip through a winter wonderland on a dog sled, you may get a taste of the excitement of mush, which is Alaska's official state sport. In Alaska, mushing is recognized as the official state sport. Even those who have never gone dog sledding before won't have any problem navigating their five-dog team through the spruce trees, over the frozen rivers, and over the tundra.

3. The Ice Art World Championships are taking place.

A competition for ice sculpture is held annually in the city of Fairbanks in the state of Alaska. This event is known as the World Ice Art Championships. Ice Alaska is an organization that does not seek to profit from its activities and was founded in 1989. Each year, more than one hundred contestants from thirty different countries take part in the competition, making it the most comprehensive sculpting competition anywhere in the globe. Tens of thousands of people go all the way to Fairbanks every year to take part in the tournament that is held there. In 1991, Ice Alaska hosted its very first ice art competition, which lasted for a total of just one week and included participation from a total of sixteen unique sculpting teams. If all goes according to plan, the event is scheduled to start in the middle of February and go all the way through March. There will be as many as seventy-five teams from all around the globe showcasing their aesthetic and technical expertise. As part of the championship, there will be a youth competition, an amateur exhibition, and three professional tournaments. In addition, there will be an amateur exhibition. Examples drawn from both real-life and abstract concepts are provided in each category.

4. Kayaking Adventures

There is nothing quite like kayaking in Alaska. The experience of paddling through icebergs and glaciers is one of a kind, and the beauty is unlike anything else you will see anywhere else in the world. Paddling through icebergs and glaciers in Alaska is one of the most beautiful places on earth. Kayaking is not only a fun way to spend time outdoors, but it's also a great way to get a good workout in and get your heart rate up.

It is not unusual to see a wide variety of Alaska's native flora and fauna when out on the water in a kayak in the state. Whales, seals, otters, porpoises, eagles, and bears are some of the animals that are often seen in this area. Because of this, you should make sure that your camera is within easy reach and get ready to catch some fantastic moments. If you are thinking about taking a trip to Alaska for vacation, renting a kayak is an excellent activity to look into doing while you are there. You may choose to rent kayaks by the hour, the day, or the week, and many companies provide deals on packages that include not only the kayaks themselves but also paddles, life jackets, and other kayaking gear. Signing up for a tour, on the other hand, will provide you with not just a guide but also all of the essential safety gear that you'll want for the excursion. This will make it the most beneficial option for you. It is also a wonderful chance to meet other people who have the same enthusiasm for kayaking as you do and to make new friends in the process.

5. Do yoga in an igloo or a geodesic dome.

The Arctic Hive is a yoga dome school that is located in the northern part of North America. It is nestled away in the stunning wilderness of the Brooks Range, which is around 275 miles away from the nearest city, and it is entirely cut off from the rest of the world. The husband and wife team of Mollie and Sean Busby are the ingenious minds behind the development of the wilderness resort known as Arctic Hive. Yoga is practiced inside a domed structure that has a diameter of twenty feet and is warmed by two separate wood fires. It takes the temperature in the room two hours to rise from ten degrees Fahrenheit to seventy degrees Fahrenheit before class, which is warm enough that you may wear a tank top while practicing yoga.

6. Give fishing through the ice a try.

Ice fishing is something that the vast majority of people have only seen depicted in movies; yet, fishermen who live in Alaska and like the sport do not allow the severe winter weather to prevent them from stepping out onto the thick, solid ice. They set up a tent, drill a hole in the ice, and wait for the fish in the water that is hidden behind the ice to take the bait they have placed in the hole. The water is rather frigid. This age-old sport in Alaska provides a chance for friends to communicate while they wait for fish, but with modern tents and heaters, it is more like a luxury party than a workday in the cold.

Ice fishing may be done on the lakes and rivers over the whole of Mainland Alaska from December through March, although it is dependent on the temperature and circumstances.

7. Examine the Iditarod to see what I mean.

As these smaller planes have the propensity to fill up quickly, fans of the Super Iditarod who are interested in viewing some of the most remote spots must make their charter bookings as soon as possible. Those people who are eager to observe how the race turns out should make their way to Nome, which is where the finish line is located. Around eight days after the beginning of the race, the race participants will begin arriving in Nome to start their trek.

8. Get some experience riding fat bikes by riding them for a while.

It's conceivable that the wheels on a fat bike seem as if they were transplanted from a motocross bike onto a standard bicycle. This is because fat bikes have larger tires than traditional bicycles. Despite their strange look, the objective of the sport is to continue playing a favorite sport despite whatever Mother Nature has in store for you. You can still have fun on the bike trails in Alaska even on a day in January when the temperature is really low if you ride a fat bike.

9. You Ought to Give Ice Skating a Try.

If you like ice skating excursions that include venturing out into the snow and pushing yourself to your limits, Alaska is the place to go. If you want to go ice skating, you could slip on your skates and stroll down to the adjacent pond, but if you're seeking a better surface, the Treadwell Ice Arena in Douglas is a nice option that you could check out instead. This is an indoor facility that provides skate rentals in addition to its reasonably priced admission fees.

Visitors who are on vacation in Anchorage have the option to spend a fun day ice skating at Portage Lake. When they skate, they can take in spectacular views of the glacier that is located nearby. Those with a daring spirit have the option of going ice skating on the glacier; however, you should be warned that the ice on the glacier isn't always in the ideal condition for skating and that conditions may change quickly.

10. Have a good time sliding down the mountain on skis or a snowboard.

When it comes to skiing, there is one thing that can be stated with complete assurance about Alaska: there will be a lot of snow. Annual snowfall totals of more than 40 feet are not uncommon in locations that are popular with tourists. These ski resorts are typical of a scale that is considered to be modest, and they provide a significant portion of their services to the skiing towns that are situated in the Anchorage and Fairbanks areas. Skiers and snowboarders are welcome to hit the slopes starting at the end of November and continuing through April.

11. Get yourself to the Fur Rendezvous as soon as possible.

In the last days of winter, the city of Anchorage plays home to the Anchorage Fur Rendezvous, which has the distinction of being both the largest and the oldest winter festival in the whole state of Alaska. For the course of the festival, participants have the option of attending either one of the 25 official activities or one of the 50 Rondy Around Town community events. Fur Rondy is the name that the locals have given to the celebration, and it has been held annually since long before Alaska was ever considered to be a state. It was originally staged in 1936 as a sports tournament that lasted for three days, and it was scheduled to coincide with the return of miners and trappers to their homes with the fruits of their labor during the winter. The event was hosted in the city of Whitehorse. Because of the participation of as many as 45 distinct philanthropic organizations, the festival has been transformed into an event that is accessible to everyone in the community.

12. Visit a Glacier

While seeing glaciers at any time of the year is a special experience, the winter months are when they come into their awe-inspiring natural beauties. It is well known that glaciers melt throughout the warmer months of the year, at which time they get covered with mud and other kinds of sediment. Throughout the winter, they often have a bright white look, and the cracks on their surface give off a stunning glacial blue light. During the summer, they typically have a bluish-green coloration. It is crucial to keep in mind that during the winter months, it is impossible to reach some glaciers, such as the Exit Glacier, due to the snow that covers the pedestrian pathways. This is something that must be kept in mind. As a result of this, I typically advise you to make use of the services of a local expert guide so that you may be provided with the right protective equipment.

AUTUMN IN ALASKA

It doesn't matter what section of the state you happen to be in during the autumn, Alaska is always going to be a wild and beautiful place that's packed with intriguing things to do. In addition, there is a wealth of things to do, such as getting the most out of the remaining summer heat or exploring the surrounding forest. A lot of people think that October is the best time to visit Alaska because it has gorgeous foliage, the sky is darker, and there are deals available since it is the "shoulder season."

1. Take a cruise around the ice fields to admire the sights.

During a glacier cruise, you will get the opportunity to take in some of the most stunning views of the natural splendor that is characteristic of the Alaskan coastline. As icebergs break apart and fall into the water, there is a probability that you may witness puffins, whales, seals, and even icebergs themselves. In addition, when you sail through the breathtaking inlets and fjords, there is a possibility that you may see wildlife, such as black bears, mountain goats, or even bald eagles. These kinds of cruises, fortunately, are among the vacations in Alaska that can be booked with the least amount of hassle. The great majority of coastal communities provide cruises as an amenity for visitors.

2. Take up fishing.

When the season of fall draws near, the days begin to become shorter, and the eggs of the salmon that hatched over the summer continue to drift down the rivers. Along the way, hungry rainbow trout and dolly varden fish consume the eggs as they float by. The decomposition of the bodies of hundreds of fish, which happens precisely as the egg frenzy is winding down, provides the food chain with a new lease of life, which in turn allows it to continue functioning normally. One of the most productive times of year to go fishing in Alaska is during the fall season. Casting for rainbow trout, Dolly Varden, grayling, steelhead, and silver salmon will seem like a breeze because fewer fishermen are competing for bites. This will cause time to pass quickly. These somewhat chillier days will envelop you in a stunning array of fall colors.

3. Attend the Alaska State Fair and have a good time there.

The annual Alaska State Fair is held in August in Palmer, which is also the venue of the fair. It is common knowledge that the fairgrounds, which are situated around an hour's drive north of Anchorage, are responsible for bringing in a sizable number of people from different regions of the state. They take part in the activity that begins at the end of August and continues for a whole week. The Fair is well-known both for its enormous veggies, which have previously held the record for largest of their kind, as well as for its breathtaking setting at the foot of the Chugach Mountains. In addition to other things, the festivities will include a range of activities such as amusement rides, food stalls, competitive demonstrations, carnival games, and live music. The whole fairgrounds are packed with free entertainment opportunities, and visitors are welcome to take part in and observe events and contests such as the rodeo, the Diaper Derby, and the Alaska Grown Games.

4. Observe the Local Fauna and Flora

The observation of the native flora and fauna is often cited as one of the most significant highlights of vacations to Alaska, and this is for several reasons. Many different species of animals and birds call the state of Alaska home, some of which include brown and black bears, moose, whales, eagles, caribou, wild sheep, and others. When you combine Alaska's beautiful and rugged landscapes, which encompass everything from high mountains to fjords and rainforests, you get a wildlife-watching experience that is unparalleled in any other location on the planet. This is because Alaska is home to a very varied collection of animal species. Although you could get a glimpse of a local animal at any time of the year, the end of the summer and the start of the fall are often the greatest times to have your camera ready. Autumn is often the last chance to observe some species before they go for the season, as bears hibernate during the winter while whales and other birds migrate to warmer waters for the winter.

Wildlife tours may help you boost your chances of seeing the species that are most important to you since animals can be located in several areas and participate in a range of activities at various times of the year. Your guides are going to be very knowledgeable about the parts of the park that provide the best chances of seeing a variety of creatures, such as bears, moose, and other kinds of wildlife.

5. Try Your Hand at Snowshoeing

You may think of snowshoeing as more of a winter activity during the colder months of the year; but, in many places of the state, you can enjoy the sport throughout the fall months as well. If you have two feet that can move, there is a significant possibility that you will be successful in your quest. Yet, this activity may seem tough at first appearance. In many of the larger cities and towns in the United States, it is possible to make a reservation for a space on a snowshoe trip. These trips often accommodate snowshoers with a wide range of degrees of competence, from novices to those with years of practice under their belts.

Several multi-use trails in the Anchorage region may be used for snowshoeing, and in some years there may even be enough snow for you to give it a try in the latter part of the fall. If you are interested in snowshoeing, you should look into the available trails. Traveling even farther north to Fairbanks is likely going to turn out to be the best option.

6. Travel throughout the state of Alaska aboard the Alaska Railroad.

The Alaska Railroad maintains regular service throughout every month of the calendar. Take the train to Fairbanks for some of the most spectacular vistas of the changing hues of fall and the chance to get up and personal with Denali. You may even take a ride on one of the few whistle-stop trains that are still operating in the United States and enjoy a day excursion up to the majestic Hurricane. Your window provides a view of the ever-changing scenery outside, which is characterized by the presence of mountains and glaciers. There is a greater possibility of coming across wild creatures. Although every route in Alaska is far more picturesque than the typical rail journey in other parts of the country, one of the most breathtaking train rides is the one that goes from Anchorage to Seward.

7. The phenomenon of seeing the Aurora Borealis

Because of the shorter days and longer nights of fall, it is the ideal time of year to see the Aurora Borealis, also known as the Northern Lights. Starting around the middle of August, visitors to the interior and Arctic parts of Alaska will be able to watch waves of green and sometimes red northern lights dancing across the sky on clear nights. This phenomenon is known as the aurora borealis. As a result of its position around 250–300 kilometers south of the Arctic Circle and year-round viewing of the aurora borealis, the city of Fairbanks has developed into a well-liked tourist destination to see the aurora borealis. While the phenomena may also be seen in more southern locales, such as Anchorage and Juneau, there are far fewer displays in these locations than there are in the northern parts of the state.

If there is a possibility that it could snow, you should bring along your camera, a tripod, and some warm clothing just in case.

8. Go Hiking

It would be an understatement to suggest that trekking in the Last Frontier is anything less than magnificent; the scenery is just breathtaking. Alaska is a huge state. It occupies almost one-third of the total land area of the 48 states that are next to it and has an area of over 660,000 square miles. It is home to two of the largest national forests in the United States as well as two-thirds of the national parklands in the United States. Moreover, it is home to two of the most popular national parks. Also, it is the location of about 78 percent of the nation's wildlife refuges. All of these are fantastic places to go hiking in the fall.

Alaska is home to one of the most varied ecosystems found in any tourism destination in the world. The southern region of this state has several fjords in addition to a temperate rainforest that has not been logged. There is a possibility of encountering both transitional and boreal forest types in the interior and south-central parts of the state of Alaska. There is a possibility that the ice tundra might be located farther north.

You may get up and personal with glaciers in a wide variety of settings spread out throughout the state. Because the tree lines are so close together, you can do alpine trekking without having to worry about height. As a result, you shouldn't put things off any longer and should instead go adventuring in the wilderness of Alaska.

9. Get yourself to Denali National Park as soon as possible.

There is a sound rationale behind the fact that more than 600,000 people go to Denali National Park on an annual basis. It is a vast national park that is both stunning and intriguing since it is home to a variety of fascinating megafauna as well as endless breathtaking views. The park should be protected as a national asset. In contrast to the vast majority of national parks, which were established with the primary purpose of conserving natural wonders, Denali was developed to maintain an ecosystem that is still capable of functioning normally. The park covers an area comparable in size to that of the state of New Hampshire and is divided in half by a road that is 92 miles in length. Mountains, glaciers, glacial valleys, boreal woods, and arctic tundra are among the features that may be found within the park's geography. There are 38 distinct species of animals, 160 different species of birds, and 758 different types of plant life that call this park home.

10. Spend some time searching for whales in the surrounding area.

Beginning in February and continuing through April each year, whales will travel from the warmer waters of Mexico to the colder waters of Alaska as part of their yearly migration. The months of May through September in Alaska are some of the best periods to see whales of a variety of species. On cruise ships, the decks are often arranged in such a way that guests may have a nice view of whales that are swimming by. If you keep your eyes open throughout the fall season, there are a few distinct species of whales that you may be able to see if you are in the right place at the right time. In the seas around Cook Inlet and Anchorage, it is possible to see beluga whales, who are distinguished by their ivory-colored skin. Throughout the late months of June and early September, people have reported seeing orcas swimming in the waters of Resurrection Bay, which is located near Seward.

If you go on a trip specifically designed for whale viewing, you will have a considerably better chance of sighting whales. The smaller boats may provide you with a better view of the whales, and if you inquire about it, your guide will most likely provide you with fascinating information on the whale pods that can be found in the region.

11. Go Hunting

The majority of Alaska's hunting seasons take place from August through October each year. The weather and activities of each season in the Last Frontier are strikingly unlike those seen in the lower 48 states. The state is the leader in the nation when it comes to the diversity of big game species that are available for hunting, which is one of the reasons why it is such a great spot to go hunting. There are many different creatures accessible for hunting, including black bears, caribou, moose, mountain goats, and muskox. Those who are interested in hunting may choose from among these options.

The hunting seasons shift from year to year, and non-resident hunters are not authorized to take part in all of the available opportunities throughout each season. It is usual practice to restrict non-residents from participating in the activity of hunting during years in which there are few or no game herds. This is done for conservation purposes.

12. The Act of Revealing the Leaves

September may provide gorgeous days with warm temperatures, making it a fantastic month for long drives or mountain excursions to take in the changing colors of the leaves. If you want to see the changing colors of the leaves, you should go in September. The lack of mosquitoes at this time of year is unquestionably one of the most significant benefits associated with the season now being experienced. The leaves of blueberry bushes convert into an eye-catching shade of red, while the leaves of birch trees turn into a stunning shade of yellow that provides a striking contrast to the dark green of the spruce trees. By the middle of September, the colors of Southcentral Alaska, which is near Anchorage, the Matanuska-Susitna Borough, and the Kenai Peninsula, begin to reach their peak and eventually achieve their full potential. The Tongass National Forest always has a vibrant green hue and may be seen close to the Inside Passage in Alaska.

Nonetheless, the falling leaves and berries of devil's club and deer cabbage generate spectacular flashes of yellow and red beneath the old-growth Sitka Spruce starting in late September and lasting through October. These flashes of color may be seen throughout the forest.

SPRINGTIME IN ALASKA

Glaciers are visible throughout the whole of Alaska's summer season, but an alarmingly high percentage of them are retreating on an annual basis. There is no better time than the spring to get up close and personal with icebergs and snow drifts than shortly before "Breakup" changes it into a muddy, slushy mess. This is the case since spring is when a "Breakup" occurs. There is no time like the spring to get up and personal with icebergs and snow drifts if that is something you are interested in doing. The information that follows is a condensed breakdown of the weather that may be expected in Alaska throughout each of the spring months.

Alaska in March

Although spring doesn't officially begin until the 21st of March, it still seems like winter to me for the whole month of March. I don't know why this is. Although it is still winter, the days are becoming longer, and the temperature is increasing, it is unlikely that you will see any tulips sprouting from the ground since it is still frozen. Despite this, there is a greater amount of sunlight. In addition to this, it is one of the two times each year when the activity of the aurora is at its highest point. The temperature in Alaska during March typically fluctuates from a low of 18 degrees Fahrenheit (-8 degrees Celsius) to a high of 34 degrees Fahrenheit (1 degree Celsius), which is far above freezing! You won't have to deal with a lot of snow in March, and you'll be able to make the most of an average of 10 hours of sunshine every day.

Alaska in April

In Alaska, the month of April is when people will start to see the first genuine indications of spring. After several months of experiencing temperatures well below freezing, Alaska experiences temperatures that range from an average low of 29 degrees Fahrenheit (-2 degrees Celsius) to an average high of 44 degrees Fahrenheit (7 degrees Celsius). These temperatures are considered to be positively warm. This event also marks the beginning of the unofficial spring season known as "Breakup," which is the time when all of the snow and ice begin to melt and the landscape becomes a complete and utter mess. The good news is that even while there is a possibility of slushy puddles and muddy conditions in April, the sky is normally clear and it does not typically snow or rain an excessive amount during this month.

Alaska in May

If you travel to Alaska in May, you will get the feeling that summer is extremely near at hand since this month marks the beginning of the true change in the seasons. If you go to Alaska in May, you will get the feeling that summer is very close at hand. Without a doubt, this is the explanation for why an increasing number of cruise lines and tour operators are beginning to provide their services earlier and earlier in May... Even though there is a whiff of winter in the air, it is starting to feel more and more like summer with each day that passes. In May, temperatures in Alaska range from a low of 4 degrees Celsius (40 degrees Fahrenheit) on average to a high of 13 degrees Celsius (55 degrees

Fahrenheit) on average (13 degrees Celsius). Although there is always a potential for late-season snow and rain, May is still a fine month to travel and is recommended as the best month to go to Alaska because of the weather. Almost half of the days on average in May are clear, making it an ideal time to go to Alaska.

1. At the Seward Brewing Company, you can get some hearty food and drink, like burgers and fries, which is a great place to go for a good time. As is the case with the cuisine of the majority of other northern (and even some extremely southern) climates, the greatest time of year to enjoy Alaskan food is when the weather is on the chillier side, such as in the spring (and autumn). After having spent my childhood in Alaska, I've found that returning there as an adult has been a lot of fun because it's allowed me to experience the flourishing craft beer scene throughout the state. After having spent my childhood in Alaska, I've found that returning there as an adult has been a lot of fun because of this opportunity. The Alaskan Brewing Company, situated in Juneau; their beers are usually delicious!, 49th State Brewery, based in Anchorage, and the Seward Brewing Company are some of the breweries that I've had the pleasure to visit and appreciate.

2. You'll discover that the overall population density is lower there.

Shoulder season travel to any destination will almost always result in a less congested experience than traveling during peak season since fewer people will be making the journey at the same time. This is just one of the many benefits that come along with visiting Alaska in the springtime, which includes several other perks.

Even a week or two before the start of the summer season, these images shot in Juneau (on the left) and

Ketchikan (on the right) highlight how desolate Alaska may seem during what is considered to be the "off" season. When I visited in May, this vista of the main pier in Juneau was devoid of any people; however, when a cruise ship pulls into the dock, it will be swarmed with people. If you want to travel to Alaska but aren't wild about the idea of squeezing past masses of people wearing white shoes, springtime is a good time to schedule a trip there since it is not as busy as other times of the year.

3. You Will See How the Alaskan Terrain Has Changed Throughout Time

My opinion is that the seasons that are considered to be "transitional" are some of the most breathtakingly beautiful that can be seen anywhere on the planet. Consider, for example, how the leaves in Vermont shed their summer green color and take on their autumn tint, or how Japan celebrates the arrival of spring with the blossoming of cherry blossoms.

Throughout the spring, Alaska gradually transitions from a location that is mostly white, black, and gray to one that is predominantly green and blue. As the season passes, waterfalls run down slopes that were before covered in snow, and the few leafy trees that were there gradually erupt into brighter and brighter green tones. (During the autumn season, the trees and leaves take on colors like red, yellow, and purple, in addition to brown, which is equivalent to the colors you'll find everywhere else in the world.) Since they serve as a continual reminder that the beauty in the world is both ephemeral and cyclical, these transitional seasons in Alaska are some of my favorites. The seasons are constantly changing, the colors are always changing, and they will return the following year.

4. Spending less money can provide you more room in your financial plan for other expenses.

Alaska Airlines

A trip to Alaska in the spring will not only enable you to take advantage of all of the other benefits that have previously been discussed, but it will also allow you to take advantage of cheap lodgings and activities. The vast majority of people postpone their trip to Alaska for several years to save up sufficient funds to spend their vacation in this "bucket list" destination. If you travel during the spring, you will be able to stretch those savings even further, which means that you may be able to extend your trip by one or two days, visit an additional location, or book an additional tour. If you travel during the spring, you will be able to stretch those savings even further.

For example, airfare for a week-long trip from Seattle to Alaska begins at just $297 per person during April and May, but on June 1st, the price quickly climbs to $350 per person for the same trip. If you do not place much importance on how much money you spend, then maybe this will not be a worry for you. If you are someone who, like me, works hard to keep to a budget and saves money whenever you have the opportunity, then coming to Alaska in the spring is an excellent way to reduce the cost of your travel expenditures.

CHAPTER 5

TOP HOSTELS IN ALASKA

Bedroom-style lodgings make it feasible to explore Alaska in a secure and cost-effective way while still taking advantage of the charming environment and feeling of community that hostels give. Bedroom-style accommodations also allow more privacy than other types of lodging.

When travelers to Alaska choose to stay in a hostel, they not only have the opportunity to interact with other tourists in the area, but also with locals who are knowledgeable about the best restaurants, tourist attractions, and other hidden gems of the state, and who can provide information that cannot be found anywhere else in the state.

1. International Spenard Hostel (Spenard Hostel)

The Spenard Hostel features a spacious plot that is furnished with a BBQ and many lawn chairs for visitors to use during the long hours of sunshine in addition to the dormitory rooms and the camping grounds. They provide more than adequate space, which includes three fully-furnished kitchens, three social spaces (one for discussion, a library for exchanging books and using computers, and a television room), and four private bathrooms designed in the form of a family bathroom. All of these amenities are included. They are committed to providing bike-sharing services in order to make it simpler for you to take advantage of the wide network of concrete cycling tracks that is spread out over the region. In the laundry that only takes pennies, the detergent is delivered at no additional charge. In addition to offering free high-speed Wi-Fi, they also provide a pay kiosk Computer for customers to use. If a customer has to leave certain goods behind while traveling throughout Alaska, they have the choice to store those items in a manner that is both cost-effective and durable in addition to having access to free compartments, which refers to space that is easily accessible.

2. Location of the Anchorage Base Camp

It's a community hostel in the neighborhood that's run by folks who like spending time in the great outdoors. Its goal is to provide a welcoming environment for people from all over the world, whether they are tourists or residents of the area. The workers like seeing different parts of Alaska and exchanging advice with one another on where to go hiking and what else there is to do. Stores such as REI and Alaska Mountaineering and Walking are located in close proximity to one another, making it easy for those who are interested in outdoor sports and need equipment for such activities to access both stores. In addition, the hotel is situated within a walking distance of fewer than five minutes from a range of bistros, cafes, live music venues, and one of the best microbreweries in the city.

3. Bent Prop Inn And Hostel Alaska

Because of the inn's central position in the city, a wide selection of shops, cafes, tourist sites, and bus shelters are all within a short walking distance from the property. Because of this, visitors are able to readily reach the city as well as the locations that are immediately around it. The Bent Prop Inn offers its visitors both private suites as well as regular rooms that are furnished with beds. In addition to having a fully equipped kitchen and bathroom, each of the private apartments also has a boudoir inside the space. Every single dormitory room has enough space to accommodate a maximum of six persons. It just takes around 10 minutes to reach Ted Stevens Anchorage International Airport whether you take a bus or a carriage there. The Alaska hostel is situated within easy walking distance of a number of well-known tourist destinations, including shopping malls, museums, and the Alaska Zoo.

4. Arctic Adventure Hostel

Midtown is where you'll find the Arctic Adventure Hostel while you're in Anchorage. From that location, Diamond Centre is 6.4 kilometers away, the downtown area of Anchorage is 3.2 kilometers away, the Alaska Zoo is 8.9 kilometers away, the Anchorage Museum is 4 kilometers away, the Alaska Native Heritage Center is 8.5 kilometers away, and Flattop Mountain is 22.5 kilometers away. It does not cost anything to use the internet, and there is no fee for parking either. In addition, we have storage areas available for rent as well as bicycles that you are welcome to use. On-site amenities include a communal kitchen that is accessible at all hours of the day and night, as well as complimentary coffee offered at a variety of times throughout the day.

5. Guesthouse in the heart of Downtown Fairbanks

The Fairbanks Downtown Hostel is located around ten kilometers from Alaska Fairbanks University and is located in the middle of the city of Fairbanks. It is possible to access the internet through free Wi-Fi both in the bedrooms and on the patio of the hotel. The establishment has both a bar and a common room for people to get together. At the hotel's restaurant, patrons have their choice of many meals that are prepared in accordance with the culinary customs of several European countries. In this hostel, every single one of the guest rooms has a contemporary television with a flat-screen display. Every accommodation has a private bathroom that is furnished with free amenities, and the bathrooms are private.

6. Billie's Backpackers Hostel

The common room of Billie's Backpackers Hostel, which is located in Fairbanks and caters to travelers on a budget, has a garden in addition to cable television. In addition to a front desk that is staffed continuously, this establishment also has a rooftop sundeck. There is a free bike rental service and free access to the internet, however, there are certain limits. The hostel has a number of social areas, in addition to a kitchen that is completely supplied, a dining area, three restrooms that each have a shower, and complimentary amenities.

7. The Guesthouse on the 9th Avenue

The core of the city of Fairbanks, where you'll find the main bus station as well as a broad choice of restaurants and pubs, is only a ten-minute walk away from our hostel, which is conveniently located in the city's downtown area. The use of the free Wi-Fi and the provision of all of the required linens is not subject to any additional fees. The 9th Avenue Hostel has both a community kitchen and a separate banquet kitchen for its guests' use. Guests are free to utilize the common area, which has a satellite television and a Blu-ray player, and there is no extra charge for their usage of this space. Bicycles are available for hire right there on the premises.

8. Sven's Basecamp Hostel & Backpackers

In the city of Fairbanks, you'll find a place called Sven's Basecamp Hostel that provides lodging options. Wi-Fi service is provided throughout the whole hotel at no additional cost to the hotel's guests. In some of the rooms, there is a sitting space that may be used for some much-needed relaxation at the end of a long and trying day. Several of the rooms have an outside space like a patio or terrace. Each room has its own private bathroom, which has either a shower or a bathtub depending on the guest's preference. The visitors have full access to the communal rooms, which consist of a television room and equipment for barbecuing. On the premises, there is a space that guests may use to keep their bags. In addition, guests are welcome to utilize the hostel's bicycles at no additional cost.

9. Alyeska Hostel

Since its opening over three decades ago, the Alyeska Hostel in Girdwood, Alaska, has provided travelers looking for low-cost overnight accommodations. In 2016, the hostel underwent a comprehensive refurbishment. You will be less than an hour away from the Anchorage airport, and you will be less than a mile away from the ski resort that is considered to be the most popular in all of Alaska. A dormitory with six bunk beds, a fully-equipped kitchen, restrooms with hot showers, and a sleeping area with space for five people are all included in the principal building. In addition to that, there is a private apartment with its own bathroom and kitchenette, as well as a cabin with its own private bathroom and kitchen. Both of these accommodations are available to guests.

10. Glacier House Hostel is a place to stay.

The rooms at the hostel all have four bunk beds, and they are quite comfy and very clean, and the prices are very reasonable. You may enjoy light-night pleasure in the summers as well as winter sports if you come here. This is an excellent location from which to plan your adventures in Alaska because they provide more than enough storage for your gear and are located close to a variety of places to shop for food and dine. Additionally, you will have access to more than enough storage for your gear at this location. There is a stop for the urban bus three blocks away from where you are now standing. Following that, you may unwind on one of the porches with some games or puzzles during the warm summer nights or during the frigid winter evenings as you view the northern lights.

THE STATE'S MOST AWARD-WINNING RESTAURANTS

Many people look to Alaska as a magnificent example of the beauty that may be found in rural places and in nature that has not been tamed. Alaska is a large state that spans the northern part of the United States. Yet, the final frontier is also home to innovative culinary creations that make use of the availability of high-quality ingredients that can be gathered from the surrounding sea and mountains. These dishes make use of the words "final frontier" and "final frontier" respectively. The bulk of Alaska has a relatively short growing season; as a direct consequence of this, fresh fruit that comes from local sources is appreciated and cooked with additional attention to detail. We take a look at 10 of the most highly regarded restaurants in the world, all of which are located in what has to be one of the most stunningly beautiful settings on the whole planet.

1. The Screaming Canopy

The restaurant and grounds of the Gustavus Inn, which were utilized with permission from the Gustavus Inn

The Crow's Nest can be found atop the Hotel Captain Cook, which is situated high above Anchorage. From this vantage point, visitors have been treated to breathtaking panoramas of the city below as well as the natural beauty that lies beyond. The Crows Nest is dedicated to providing its customers with an unforgettable dining experience. Each of the restaurant's chefs has had a classical education and infuses their cuisine with a very French sensibility. The top cuts of dry-aged beef, scallops from the surrounding region, and game meats that have been masterfully cooked may all be found on the menu here. The elk loin, which is the house's specialty, goes well with the turnips and carrot puree that is served beside it. The only meal that is offered at Crow's Nest is dinner, and it is strongly recommended that reservations be made in advance.

2. Gustavus Inn

When a restaurant offers a bush plane as one of the modes of transportation to get to the location of the restaurant, it is a clear indication that the dining experience there is something special. The Gustavus Inn is both a hotel and a restaurant, and it can be found inside a national park that is just approximately 60 kilometers away from Juneau, the capital of the state of Alaska. The guests reside in a historic home that is situated on the site, and the dining room is where they eat their meals while they are there. Those who are hungry may anticipate eating salmon and crab that were caught in the strait that is close to the property, in addition to the food that was collected fresh that day from the garden that is situated on the site. Expect more than just your run-of-the-mill fare at Gustavus; the James Beard Foundation has recognized the restaurant for its outstanding culinary offerings, so don't base your expectations just on its rural setting.

3. Homestead Restaurant

The Homestead Restaurant is a buried gem that can only be found by traveling far into the interior regions of Alaska. Since it opened over half a century ago, this restaurant has been an important part of the Homer community, and the people who own it are always pleased to meet new customers. The farmhouse routinely catches fresh fish and other marine delicacies from the ocean that is nearby and prepares them in an uncomplicated manner in order to maximize their flavor. Oysters served on the half shell, shrimp cakes, and cioppino stew are just a few of the seafood options that are available on the regular menu. The Homestead boasts a wide menu of vegetarian choices, which are guaranteed to please even the pickiest of customers. Because of this, the restaurant is a perfect choice for anyone who would prefer not to order seafood. You are only permitted to do so when the weather is warmer.

4. Foraker

The Talkeetna Lodge, which acts as the base camp for mountaineers trying to conquer Mount McKinley, the highest peak in North America, is home to the Foraker restaurant. Mount McKinley is the highest peak in North America. Visitors are able to take in stunning views of the mountain's most impressive top while staying securely distant from the dangers of real mountain climbing in the posh atmosphere of the Foraker restaurant. Fresh seafood is something that tourists to Alaska have come to expect from the restaurants in the state. Some examples of fresh seafood dishes are halibut filets cooked on the grill and Alaskan king crab legs that have been steamed. In addition, the raspberry rhubarb sauce that is provided with the duck that was found locally and presented with it is a customer favorite.

5. Knik

The amazing landscape can be seen from Seven Glaciers, which was generously provided by Alyeska Resort.

Those who are searching for interesting and novel experiences will find that the Knik River Lodge is the perfect place to stay. The resort offers its visitors the opportunity to participate in a variety of exhilarating activities, such as glacier dog sledding and helicopter trips. When the visitors have worked up an appetite, the lodge's restaurant is the perfect location for them to go to unwind while enjoying a meal that has been meticulously prepared by the lodge's chefs. A yurt is a unique structure that resembles a round tent made of canvas and serves as the restaurant's location. A yurt is a building that houses an eatery. The yurt is decked up with luxury furnishings, such as cushy sofas and subdued lighting. The menu is changed to match what is presently fresh and in season, but the options of cedar-planked salmon and prime rib continue to be favorites among customers regardless of the changes. The Knik River Lodge does not in any manner have a dress code unless you consider the snow boots and parka that you are required to wear if you travel there during the winter. Other than that, there is no dress code. Other than that, absolutely anybody and everyone are free to come and go as they choose.

6. Seven Glaciers

Even before entering the actual facility, visitors are treated to a one-of-a-kind experience afforded to them by the position of Seven Glaciers, which is perched atop the highest point of Alyeska Resort. This restaurant can only be accessed by taking a gondola ride up the side of the mountain, which is a journey that both customers and staff members are required to undergo in order to join the establishment. After you have arrived at Seven Glaciers, the dining room will take your breath away with its amazing views of the wild and beautiful nature of Alaska. Yet, after that, the magnificent meal you've been enjoying won't be done yet. The food at the restaurant is sophisticated and befitting of some form of celebration, and the service at the restaurant is unmatched by any other establishment in the city. The fish is cooked using the freshest ingredients available, and all of the veggies come from local growers in the surrounding vicinity. There is no shadow of a doubt that Seven Glaciers makes the utmost use of all that this state has to offer.

7. Jack Sprat

Jack Sprat is a peaceful little town that always has enormous things going through its head. The restaurant was founded on the premise of catering to a broad range of client's interests and preferences by taking inspiration from a variety of cultures and regions all over the globe. Meals that may be enjoyed by vegetarians are not an afterthought but rather a highly valued component of the menu at this establishment. The carnivorous meals provided at Jack Sprat are proudly made using locally caught fish that was harvested in a sustainable way and meat that was raised in a humane manner. In addition, the restaurant has a stellar reputation across the little ski town for the mouthwatering breakfast it serves. Since the crew is formed of individuals who have traveled extensively and place a high emphasis on diversity, this restaurant is an appealing refuge that welcomes patrons from out of town in addition to the regulars who frequent it on a regular basis.

8. Crush

Crush is a restaurant in Anchorage that is dedicated to offering exceptional food and wine, and it has earned a reputation for having a wine collection that is among the finest in the world. The restaurant's name, Crush, comes from the word "crush," which means "to crush" or "to crush" anything. The passion that the restaurant has shown for wine in recent years has led to the development of a retail wine shop on the second level, just over the dining area. The creation of delicacies such as the elk and pig meatloaf, the arugula salad with melon and red wine feta, and the truffled white beans has garnered a cult of loyal devotees while seeming to be deceptively basic. The menu at this restaurant is purposely restricted since the institution lays a major focus on providing high-quality dishes that may be properly paired with a broad choice of superb wines. The restaurant also has a large selection of wines from across the world.

9. Ginger

The number of restaurants in Anchorage is growing, which means that foodies have a growing number of options to choose from that are of high quality. Because of the substantial amount of Asian influence that it has, ginger stands out from other spices. The up-to-date and immaculate interior design gives it an air of sophistication while yet maintaining a homey atmosphere. On the menu at Ginger, you'll find not only traditional dishes like lettuce wraps and sushi rolls but also more forward-thinking options like banana and lemongrass soup and baked sea scallop macaroni and cheese. Traditional dishes like lettuce wraps and sushi rolls can be found on the menu at Ginger. In addition to a discerning selection of sales and wines, the bar has a broad selection of hand-crafted beers from nearby breweries. The restaurant is also open for breakfast and lunch, and during those meals, it provides breakfast and lunch cuisine that is an inventive spin on standard American fare.

CHAPTER 6

NIGHTLIFE IN ALASKA

1. The Salty Dawg Bar and Restaurant

The Salty Dog Saloon in Alaska is the perfect destination to enjoy a night out on the town. This saloon, which can be located in Homer, Alaska, is the perfect place to spend an evening packed with laughter-inducing activities such as dancing, drinking, and listening to music. Because of its warm and inviting atmosphere as well as its excellent selection of regional drinks, the Salty Dog Saloon is certain to be the most memorable part of your evening. The Salty Dog Margarita, the establishment's signature drink and namesake, is the one that brings in the most customers. This mouthwatering drink will undoubtedly get you buzzed due to the handmade margarita mix that it contains. If you're looking for something with a little bit less alcohol in it, you may have a cold beer or a specialty cocktail instead. The friendly bartenders are happy to provide advice and recommendations to help you choose the perfect drink to complement your evening.

Every evening, patrons may also enjoy live music when they visit the Salty Dawg Saloon. This pub has something for everyone, from rock to country, and everything in between. You may have a nice time with your buddies when you let loose to your favorite music and dance the night away. In addition to live music and a selection of drinks, the Salty Dawg Saloon hosts a variety of enjoyable events for its customers. You have the option to play video games, compete in a game of pool or darts, or join an existing game. Even better, you get the opportunity to compete for prizes by taking part in the weekly trivia night that they host.

2. The Arctic Slaughterhouse

The Arctic Bar in Alaska is a wonderful place to spend the evening if you find yourself in that state. The bar, which can be found in the center of downtown Anchorage, is well-known for the lively atmosphere it maintains, as well as for the outstanding drinks and delectable cuisine it serves. The bar offers a broad range of craft beers, cocktails, and beers, in addition to a comprehensive selection of wine from all over the world. The Arctic Bar has both an inside lounge area as well as an outside terrace for patrons so they can relax and have a good time while they are there. The Arctic Bar is known for having some of the best live music in town. In the bar, live music is performed by a variety of groups and solo artists each night. Anything from solo acoustic sets to big bands playing rock can be accomplished with this. There is no question that you will delight in the music for the whole evening. There are also other things to do, such as pool tables, to keep everyone entertained and engaged.

In the Arctic Bar, there is a wide variety of nocturnal entertainment options available. Players have access to a wide variety of board games in addition to the available arcade games. In addition, there is a space for visitors to sing their hearts out in the form of karaoke.

3. The Saloon of the Red Dog

The Red Dog Saloon is well-recognized as one of the most popular spots for nightlife in Alaska. The Red Dog Saloon, which is located in the heart of downtown Anchorage, is an excellent establishment at which to while away an evening taking in live music, indulging in some delectable food, and sampling a variety of drinks. The Red Dog Saloon, which is easily recognized because of its bright red neon sign, has been a long-time favorite among the community. It is the perfect venue for both locals and tourists to experience some of the best nightlife the state has to offer. During their time at The Red Dog Saloon, guests have the opportunity to take part in a variety of activities. There is live music playing all the time, ranging from rock and roll to blues and country, and guests may take advantage of numerous different karaoke events every night of the week. In addition, the bar has for its clientele a pool table and a jukebox that plays a range of songs both from the present day and from the past.

The Red Dog Saloon offers a range of food and drinks to its customers in addition to its other services. The bar offers a comprehensive menu of classic pub fares such as burgers, sandwiches, and appetizers in addition to a wide selection of specialized beers, wines, and cocktails. In addition to the typical events that take place there, the pub often hosts live music performances, trivia nights, and stand-up comedy acts.

4. Lavelle's Taphouse

Lavelle's Taphouse is recognized as one of the most popular destinations in Alaska for nightlife. It is a quaint institution that can be found in the middle of Anchorage, and it is well-known for its friendly personnel as well as the extensive beverage selection that it offers. In addition to a wide variety of mouthwatering dishes, the bar has an extensive menu of alcoholic beverages such as beers, wines, and cocktails. In Lavelle's Taphouse, one of the most captivating activities is the live music that is offered. The music that is played inside the bar is usually vibrant and exciting, and it involves a variety of bands from both the local area and from farther afield. Because of the living environment, which is often filled with laughter and conversation, it is an excellent spot for getting to know new people and spending a night out with friends. Karaoke, pool, darts, and weekly quiz nights are just some of the additional activities that may be enjoyed at this bar, in addition to the ample space available for dancing and mingling with other patrons. At Lavelle's Taphouse, guests of all ages will be able to discover something that they like, and they won't have to pay for an arm and a leg to have a good time there.

5. The Yukon Bar and Grill

The Yukon Bar is a favored destination for locals as well as visitors in Alaska due to its well-known reputation for having a lively evening scene. The bar, which can be found in the heart of Anchorage, makes available a wide variety of opportunities for activities and forms of amusement. Guests can take use of live music, karaoke, and DJs in addition to the extensive drink variety that is offered. In addition, there are pool tables, quiz nights, and a jukebox with a variety of music that guests may enjoy. Since the atmosphere is playful and animated at the same time, it is an excellent choice for a night out on the town. In addition, The Yukon Bar serves mouthwatering pub food with a unique spin. On the menu, you'll find a selection of traditional bar food such as burgers, wings, and nachos in addition to some creative takes on pub classics such as loaded fries, fish tacos, and mac and cheese bites. Beer and beverages, including regional craft beers and specialty mixed cocktails, are just some of the options available at this bar's extensive beverage menu.

In addition to its exciting nightlife, the Yukon Bar also hosts a variety of unique events and activities. Live music performances, stand-up comedy shows, and quiz nights are held there regularly.

6. The Fairview Inn and Suites

It is common knowledge that the Fairview Hotel is the place to go for nightlife in Alaska. The inn, which can be found in the lively city of Anchorage, gives visitors access to a variety of different forms of entertainment and has a location that is unique in its own right. At the Fairview Inn, everyone is welcome to enjoy the live music, DJs, and comedy performances.

The inn has a décor that is a fusion of modern and rustic styles, and it's warm and inviting atmosphere has made it a popular hangout spot for the locals. In the bar, you may choose from a wide variety of alcoholic beverages, including beers, wines, and specialty cocktails. After a long and challenging day, the restaurant is a great place to reward oneself with a satisfying meal since it serves mouthwatering food and has an elegant ambiance. Guests at the Fairview Hotel who prefer to remain out till the wee hours of the morning may choose from a selection of exciting entertainment options. Guests get the opportunity to take part in karaoke, themed nights, and quiz evenings. A dancing floor is available for your use at the bar, allowing you to show off your moves as you enjoy yourself.

7. Restaurant and Sports Bar Fat Stan's specializes in Pizza.

The Fat Stan's Sports Bar and Pizzeria are one of the most well-known places to go out for a night in the town in Alaska. This restaurant, which can be found in the city of Anchorage, is well-liked by both locals and visitors to the area. Because of the warm, inviting, and friendly atmosphere, it is an excellent location in which to relax and have a good time for yourself. In the bar, patrons may choose from a wide variety of alcoholic beverages, including beers, wines, and cocktails, as well as a selection of hors d'oeuvres and pizzas. You have the option of selecting pizzas with toppings that are more common or pizzas with toppings that are entirely original and can't be found anywhere else. Burgers and sandwiches are only a few examples of the many other options that may be found on the menu. The staff is friendly and happy to help you in making the best choice for either your meal or beverage at all times.

In addition to these activities, the bar also has karaoke nights, pool and darts competitions, and trivia nights. DJs and live music performances are presented every day of the week at Fat Stan's.

8. Chilkoot Charlie's is the place to go.

Chilkoot Charlie's is a well-known nightlife attraction in Alaska that offers a diverse assortment of enjoyable activities. In addition to having a comprehensive selection of drinks and appetizers, it is also well known for the live music, dancing, and other events that it hosts. A bar is an excellent area for groups to meet and have a good time because of its size and the plenty of seating it provides.

Karaoke evenings, beer tastings, and live music performances are just some of the events that are often hosted at the bar, which is known for its diverse array of activities. In addition, they have a patio outdoors that is perfect for use in the evenings throughout the summer as well as an upper space that can be reserved for private events.

In addition to a list of specialty cocktails, the bar has a selection of alcoholic beverages such as beers, wines, and spirits. It offers a broad array of cuisine, including some of the best things that Alaska has to offer, such as king crab and reindeer sausage. Because of its warm and friendly staff, Chilkoot Charlie's is a popular site for tourists who want to acquire a feel for the culture of the area they are visiting. Also, it has a convenient location in the middle of Anchorage, which makes it easy to get to and from the hotel.

9. The pub located inside the Bear Tooth Theatre

At the Bear Tooth Theatre Pub in Anchorage, Alaska, the pleasures of a restaurant and bar are mixed with the utility of a movie theater for the utmost convenience. One of the most well-liked places in Alaska for nightlife, this cutting-edge concept first opened its doors in the year 2002.

The cinema presents a diverse assortment of movies, ranging from up-and-coming indie productions to time-honored classics. A variety of food and drink options, ranging from classic pub fare to more adventurous alternatives, are available for patrons to choose from inside the establishment. In the bar, you can get a range of regional craft beers in addition to a selection of specialty beverages.

In addition to being a theater and a bar, Bear Tooth also hosts a variety of live performances, some of which include musical acts, burlesque shows, and comedic performances. In addition, during the year, the theater hosts several one-of-a-kind events, such as movie marathons and pub quizzes.

The atmosphere at Bear Tooth is friendly and unhurried. The atmosphere is warm and inviting, and the staff is quite kind. As it is family-friendly, the venue does not prohibit children from attending any of the acts or activities that take place there.

10. The bar of the Triangle Club

One of the most well-known spots for nightlife in Alaska is the Triangle Club Bar. It offers a wide variety of entertainment opportunities, such as dancing, live music, and pool tables, among other things. In addition to delicious food, the bar offers a large selection of alcoholic and non-alcoholic drinks, such as craft beer, wine, and cocktails. Those who want to relax and have a good time during the evening may take advantage of the spacious bar area, the ample seating, and the warm atmosphere.

Because it plays home to a variety of events and activities, the pub is an excellent location to visit. Every Thursday night, they host a karaoke night where patrons may showcase their vocal prowess and sing along to their favorite songs. On Tuesday nights, there are also trivia competitions where you may test your knowledge on a variety of topics. These competitions take place every week. If you are looking for something to do outside of the bar, you can find all you want at Triangle Club Bar. They provide a variety of outdoor activities, such as fishing, hiking, and skiing, to its guests. As there are many different ski slopes in the area, you may want to take a break from the bar and participate in some winter sports instead.

11. The saloon was known as Ernie's Old Time

The best of Alaskan nightlife can be found at Ernie's Old Time Saloon, which also offers a one-of-a-kind experience for anyone interested in Alaska nightlife. Because of its location in the heart of Anchorage, it offers visitors and locals alike a once-in-a-lifetime opportunity to enjoy a truly unique and unforgettable experience. The atmosphere at Ernie's is perfect for a night out with a significant other or a group of close friends. The atmosphere at the pub is warm and inviting, and it is cozy yet unhurried at the same time. The saloon provides its customers with a bar as well as many tables at which they may dine and drink. The bar is known for its extensive selection of craft beers, wines, and cocktails, in addition to its menu of food that is both simple and delicious.

Ernie's is a great spot to go to have some fun. The pub has live music seven days a week, and it also often hosts karaoke nights. In addition to these events, the pub is also the site of a variety of other celebrations and activities, such as themed holiday parties, pool tournaments, and trivia evenings.

12. The Brewery of the Weird Man Rush

The Odd Man Rush Brewery is an excellent option for a nightlife destination for folks who live in

Alaska or who will be visiting the state. Anchorage offers visitors the opportunity to have a unique and entertaining experience, making it the ideal site for those looking for such a place. The brewery not only offers the beers that it makes on the premises but also a variety of craft beers and ales produced by other local and regional brewers. The atmosphere is laid back, warm, and inviting thanks to the presence of several board games, retro arcade games, and a wonderful jukebox in the background.

There are a lot of unique events that take place at the brewery, such as evenings centered on beer and oysters, nights devoted to music and beer, and events that focus on beer sampling from casks. If you're looking for something a little less hectic, there are regular trivia nights and open mic nights for artists who want to showcase their talents. The food selection at Odd Man Rush Brewery is outstanding and features a range of creative dishes that are produced using regionally sourced and freshly prepared ingredients. In addition to the standard pub cuisine such as fish and chips and nachos, they also offer more unique options such as reindeer sliders and smoked salmon and rice bowls. In addition, the dining selection offers options that are suitable for vegans and those who avoid gluten.

If you are looking to have a good time on a night out in Alaska, Odd Man Rush Brewery is a great place to go. They serve delicious beer and have a fun atmosphere. Spend some quality time with the people you care about while indulging in some delectable food and beverages. You won't quickly forget the experience, that's for sure.

SOME NATIVE FESTIVALS AND EVENTS

FEBRUARY---

Festival Séet Ká | Petersburg

a festival celebrating indigenous peoples with the goal of fostering cultural awareness and revival among the Séet Ká Kwáan community's indigenous population.

Messenger Feast | Kivgiq | Anchorage

The Kivgiq, also known as the Messenger Feast, is held once every two years and brings together locals from all across the region. This multi-day event, which normally takes place at the beginning of February, is vital to the way of life of the local community and incorporates traditional dance.

MARCH

The Iditarod Sled Dog Race and an Art Show To Be Held in Anchorage

Iditarod Trail Sled Dog Race is the name of an annual dog sledding competition that takes place from Anchorage to Nome and back again. Attend the Iditarod Art Show taking place the same week!

The Festival of Native Arts is held in Fairbanks every year.

The Festival of Native Arts encourages cross-cultural communication and comprehension via the mediums of traditional Indian dance, music, and arts.

The Cama-i Dance Festival held by Bethel

The Yukon Delta is widely regarded as the most important cultural and artistic performance event in the region.

APRIL

Sports that are Traditionally Played in Northern Regions | Juneau

Classic athletic competitions such as the kneel leap, wrist carry, and Alaskan high kick are taken part in by students from junior high schools and senior high schools.

The Native American Youth Olympics are held in Anchorage (NYO)

Ten of the competitions that are part of the NYO Games, which first took place in 1972, are modeled after games that Alaska Native people played in previous eras to evaluate their potential for survival.

The Day for the Legacy of Culture

The objectives of this day are to raise awareness about the diversity and precariousness of cultural heritage and to acknowledge the significance of cultural heritage in our everyday lives.

June is the month of the Anchorage Urban Unangax Culture Camp.

People of all ages are able to increase their understanding of the Unangax way of life by participating in participatory cultural events and by interacting with members of the Unangax community. The ancient Unangax customs are revised so that they are compatible with the way we live today, which enriches the lives of those who take part in cultural activities.

Spring Whaling Festival: Nalukataq | Utqiagvik

With the end of the whale-hunting season in the spring, the Iupiat people observe their festival of Nalukataq. Together with a blanket toss, traditional music, and dances are performed throughout this event.

JULY

Native Alaskan musicians and dancers came together during the Midnight Sun Intertribal Powwow in Fairbanks to play traditional drums, sing, and dance, all in the spirit of celebrating the community and expressing appreciation.

Fairbanks serves as the host city for the World Eskimo Native Olympic Games.

The WEIO games demonstrate how important it is to be well-prepared in order to survive. They require ability in addition to physical strength, physical agility, and physical endurance. In this manner, the people who live in northeast Alaska teach their children that in order to be self-sufficient, they must have the ability to be resilient no matter what challenges they face. In the games, any part of the body was fair game.

Indigenous Peoples Day | Observed Throughout the State in the Month of October

This day honors Native Americans in the United States for their contributions to the nation's past, present, and future. The festival places an emphasis on the history as well as the consequences that colonialism had on Indian communities. In addition to recognizing the traditions, achievements, and perseverance of current Native peoples, the holiday also acknowledges the legacy of colonialism.

Quyana Alaska | Fairbanks and Anchorage

This cultural event has been held by the Alaska Federation of Natives (AFN) for many years, and it has aided in the preservation and restoration of traditional dances. The term "thank you" in Yup'ik is "Quyana."

NOVEMBER

The month is dedicated to celebrating Alaska Native History throughout the state

This month is a time to celebrate the rich and diverse cultures, practices, and histories of Alaska Native People while also honoring the major achievements that have been achieved by Alaska Native People.

Made in the USA
Las Vegas, NV
09 January 2024

84125754R00114